The Dark Side of Family Communication

Key Themes in Family Communication

Douglas L. Kelley, *Marital Communication*

Katheryn C. Maguire, *Stress and Coping in Families*

Loreen N. Olson, Elizabeth A. Baiocchi-Wagner, Jessica M. W. Kratzer, Sarah E. Symonds, *The Dark Side of Family Communication*

Thomas J. Socha and Julie Yingling, *Families Communicating with Children*

The Dark Side of Family Communication

Loreen N. Olson,
Elizabeth A. Baiocchi-Wagner,
Jessica M. W. Kratzer,
and Sarah E. Symonds

polity

First published in 2012 by Polity Press

Polity Press
65 Bridge Street
Cambridge CB2 1UR, UK

Polity Press
350 Main Street
Malden, MA 02148, USA

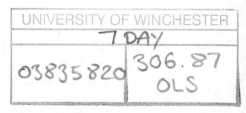
ISBN-13: 978-0-7456-4797-5 (hardback)
ISBN-13: 978-0-7456-4798-2 (paperback)

A catalogue record for this book is available from the British Library.

Typeset in 11 on 13 pt Sabon
by Servis Filmsetting Ltd, Stockport, Cheshire
Printed and bound in Great Britain by MPG Books Group Ltd, Bodmin, Cornwall

The publisher has used its best endeavors to ensure that the URLs for external websites referred to in this book are correct and active at the time of going to press. However, the publisher has no responsibility for the websites and can make no guarantee that a site will remain live or that the content is or will remain appropriate.

Every effort has been made to trace all copyright holders, but if any have been inadvertently overlooked the publisher will be pleased to include any necessary credits in any subsequent reprint or edition.

For further information on Polity, visit our website: www.politybooks.com

Contents

Figures and Tables

Prologue

Vangelisti (2004) noted that "the family is the crucible of society" (p. ix). As such, the family system is a key site where lives are formed, developed, and changed across time. For many, their lives are nurtured and sustained by their families, providing them with a source of security, comfort, and support. Unfortunately, however, many others may find that their family system is a site of much pain, suffering, stress, maltreatment, and perhaps even abuse. Statistics support such claims. For instance, the Family Violence Prevention Fund (2010) reports that more than fifteen million children in the United States live in families in which partner violence occurred at least once in the past year; and 61 percent of homeless girls and 19 percent of homeless boys reported experiencing sexual abuse prior to leaving home. Sadly, 93 percent of sexual assault and rape cases that occur in children under twelve are carried out by someone they know, and 34 percent of these cases by someone in the family (RAINN, 2010).

The communicative aspects of these darker sides of family life are the focus of our book entitled *The Dark Side of Family Communication*. According to Spitzberg and Cupach (1994), "the dark side metaphor is useful for understanding interpersonal relationships because it focuses on important, yet neglected, phenomena and helps to discern new and useful connections among concepts" (p. 315). Due in part to some authors' (Duck, 1994; Spitzberg & Cupach, 1994) push for applying a darker lens to relationship studies, numerous scholars have answered the call, investigating areas such as teasing and bullying (Kowalski, 2007), jealousy and envy (Guerrero & Anderson, 1998a, 1998b), relational partner violence (Lloyd & Emery, 1999; Olson, 2002a, 2002b), and parent–child violence (Eckstein, 2004; Morgan & Wilson, 2007) – both in face-to-face relationships and in cyberspace (Whitty, 2007).

With what appears to be an unending string of dark topics, scholars intrigued with the dark side of relationships are rarely without subject matter. However, the plethora of potential research areas gives way to the problem of dark side boundary management. For instance, although most would agree that certain topics (e.g., family violence) would fall into a darker category, what about topics that blur dark and bright (e.g., a marriage strengthened by conflict)? What is the common denominator in all that is dark? Ironically, the "dark side of relationships" metaphor can be described best as a "gray" area. Scholars' theorizing about the dark side of communication in interpersonal literature ranges from merely overlooked or obscured topic areas (e.g., Spitzberg & Cupach, 1994) to the sabotaging, spoiling, or quotidian hassles of relationships (Duck, 1994).

Narrowing the focus of the metaphor to one particular area of relationship study (e.g., the family) only exacerbates the problem. While many publications have focused on the broader domain of interpersonal and family relationships, to the best of our knowledge articulating a theoretical framework for understanding the dark side of *family* communication has yet to be undertaken. Of course, this is not to say that family communication scholars have been completely deterred from studying darker aspects of family life. Researchers have looked into various negativities in the family system, including sibling violence (Eriksen & Jensen, 2006), jealousy (Aune & Comstock, 2002), depression (Paolucci & Violato, 2004; Straus, 1996), child and elder abuse (Barnett, Miller-Perrin, & Perrin, 2005; Jacobson, Gottman, Waltz, Rushe, Babcock, & Holtzworth-Munroe, 1994), adolescent-to-parent abuse (Eckstein, 2004, 2007), critiques of "normal" family interaction (Stafford & Dainton, 1994), conflict and power struggles (Sillars, Canary, & Tafoya, 2004: Solomon, Knobloch, & Fitzpatrick,

2004) and spousal abuse (Olson, 2004; Stamp & Sabourin, 1995).

Yet, even with the diversity of scholarship, we arrive at where we began: how does one theorize – comprehensively – the dark side of communication within the family? Given the powerful influence of the family on one's self, one's familial relationships, and one's non-familial relationships (Vangelisti, 2004), exploring this area in a way that *highlights interconnections between macro-level and micro-level theorizing* is merited. As we noted, communication scholars have conducted a good deal of research on the dark side of family communication, but have yet to weave together theoretical conceptualizations. Thus, a major goal of this book is to present a definition and perspective that articulate the systemic and specific factors associated with the dark side of family communication. In Chapter 6, we combine the material summarized in the earlier chapters into what we call the Darkness Model of Family Communication. We assert that the model will enhance the examination of family communication by (a) thoroughly examining the interdependent levels and factors involved in dark family communication, and (b) providing a unifying theoretical framework for family communication researchers and/or practitioners.

Specifically, this book discusses major research on the dark side of family communication organized in such a way as to elucidate the processes involved in the construction, processing, and effects of dark messages within the family system. *The Dark Side of Family Communication* integrates research and theories that explore the communicative "shades of darkness" within family systems and elucidates how a positivity/negativity dialectic (Duck, 1994; Spitzberg & Cupach, 1998) may be present in many, albeit not all, of these processes. For example, as noted by Stafford and Dainton (1994), "normal," ordinary families experience darker interactions from time to time. Conversely, healthy interactions exist within dysfunctional or unhealthy families. In addition to reviewing research and theory on the more common dark familial processes (e.g., intimate violence, incest, and sibling violence), this text also relies on scholarship that illuminates how some dark interactions between family members may co-exist alongside positive ones or may function in both positive and negative ways. We also explore the darkness dynamic at a social level, examining more specifically, the role of religion, politics, and the media on the social construction and enactment of family life in the United States.

Each chapter of *The Dark Side of Family Communication* will include a narrative of a fictional family experiencing the dynamics explained in the chapter. The reader will be introduced to the Moore family in the first chapter and will read more about the members and their communication interactions in subsequent chapters. Each narrative entry will build upon the previous, paralleling the interlocking, interdependent nature of the material reviewed in the chapters. This unique feature is utilized to bring the theory and research alive for you, the reader. Finally, discussion questions at the end of each chapter are presented as a means of facilitating discussion and generating ideas for further consideration.

In closing, we think it is important to acknowledge that studying the dark side of family communication has the potential to stir emotions within us, to illicit thoughts and memories of interactions we wish to forget, or to judge others negatively for living in a dark family environment. In fact, the potential for such negativity may prompt one to ask how could we, as dark side scholars, dedicate our intellectual energies to the darker side of human life? Without a doubt, each of us has asked that question of ourselves at least once. Our response to this "why" question is, because it matters so much. Our families form the bedrock of our existence. As noted by Floyd and Mormon (2006), families "enjoy a level of permanence unparalleled by almost anything else in our lives . . . the family is situated at the focal point of nearly all relational encounters. It is, truly, a masterpiece of human experience" (p. xi). With family playing such a prominent role in our lives, we believe it is essential to understand it in its entirety – warts and all. We hope that you too will come to see the value in studying family foibles, anticipating that such knowledge can increase the likelihood of more family follies.

Prologue

Like any true research project, this book could not have been completed without the assistance of family, friends, and colleagues, who have supported us through this adventure. As a group, the authors would like to thank: Wanjiru Mbure, an original author and contributor to the Darkness Model (described more fully in subsequent chapters); our editor (Andrea Drugan) and the staff of Polity books; and the scholars who are cited throughout the book whose research has made this project possible. We would also like to thank the anonymous reviewers of earlier versions of our Darkness Model and our book proposal, whose contributions we found of great assistance.

Finally, each author would like to thank individually those who supported us throughout this endeavor.

- I would like to extend a heartfelt thanks to my biggest fan and life partner, Mark Fine. His patience, combined with his own expertise in family studies, were qualities often tapped during the writing of this book. Thanks, too, to my forever babies, Kenyon and Keaton, who show me the brightness of family life; to Julia and Aubrey who have taught me that through family challenges comes a deeper sense of purpose, togetherness, and love; and to Freud, Einstein, and Foucault, my four-legged children, who reinforce the positivity–negativity dialectic of family life. Finally, I want to express gratitude to my family-of-origin, Bonnie, Cliff, LesLee, and Lana, whose love and support always makes me stronger. ~LNO

- I would like to acknowledge my partner, David Wagner, who, as a family clinical psychologist, often acted as my sounding board and devil's advocate throughout much of the brainstorming and writing process. I am continually amazed and inspired by his abilities to restore hope and happiness to the families he works with and can only hope that this book contributes a fraction of what he contributes every day. His support and encouragement of my work never falter. Furthermore, in writing these pages, it is impossible to not reflect on my own family and the bond we share. Tom, Rhonda, and Kaitlin are the best parents and sister a person could hope for – I'm so grateful for your love and all the "brightness" you continue to bring to my life. ~EBW

- I would like to thank my husband, partner, and best friend, Matt, for his continued love, support, and patience throughout my academic career and in all parts of life. To my daughter, Jemma, who kicked me during some of the final writing of this project – thank you for being the most precious person in my life and for making me smile every time I see you. I want to thank my parents (Tim and Malia Wilson), my brother and his family (Adam, Kerri, Carter, and Molly Wilson), and all of my family and friends. I would not be where I am today without their support, love, and good humor. I would also like to thank my chihuahua, Scrappy, who sat with me during most of the research and writing of this project and all others. Finally, I want to thank my co-authors for creating a team that worked so well together. Specifically, to Dr. Olson, thank you for inviting me to write this book with you and, as always, I appreciate your continued guidance and mentorship. ~JK
- I would like to thank my parents, Peter and Dolly, for leaving me alone during my magic writing spells; my sisters, Abby and Emily, for providing insightful ideas for me to chew on; my niece, Lily, for making sure I got my "homework" done, so I could play with her; my partner Matt for holding my hand; and those extended family members who shed light on a lot of the dark ideas presented in this book. ~SES

1

Conceptualizing the "Dark Side" of Family Communication

with Wanjiru Mbure

Author Alex Haley once said, "In every conceivable manner, the family is our link to our past, our bridge to our future" ("Great Inspirational Quotes," 2010). These words reveal what so many individuals know – our families provide the glue that connects all the parts of our lives – for better and for worse. For some of us, the bonds are strong, enduring, and constant. For others, the connections are fractured and non-existent. For still others, the linkages are both inconsistent and resilient.

Regardless of the strength of our familial bond, most would concur that our families play a significant role in the construction of our identities. Families are primary socializing agents (Burleson & Kunkel, 2002; Kunkel, Hummert, & Dennis, 2006; Medved, Brogan, McClanahan, & Morris, 2006), teaching children, for instance, the difference between right and wrong, the (im)proper ways to communicate, and the best ways to show love and respect. Families also teach us how to communicate hate and prejudice (Bonilla-Silva, 2006), to communicate anger and hostility (Vangelisti, Maguire, Alexander, & Clark, 2007), and to behave deleteriously (Prescott & Le Poire, 2002). Importantly, the family is a living organism, constantly changing and growing. The socialization that takes place is equally dynamic and enduring. Thus, one is constantly impacted by the family as an organic system – adults and youth alike. As such, the social unit known as the family becomes an important site to focus scholarly attention because of its tenacious, yet shifting ability to impact individuals across their lifespans.

One cannot ignore that an element of families' enduring nature is their darker moments. Writers, poets, comics, and therapists alike have spoken of the challenges and struggles of family life. The textbox below contains a sampling of such philosophizing.

In each family a story is playing itself out, and each family's story embodies its hope and despair. Auguste Napier ("Wisdom Quotes," 2010a)

If you cannot get rid of the family skeleton, you may as well make it dance. George Bernard Shaw (as cited in Peters, 1996)

Happy families are all alike; every unhappy family is unhappy in its own way. Leo Tolstoy (1873/2004)

Family quarrels are bitter things. They don't go by any rules. They're not like aches or wounds; they're more like splits in the skin that won't heal because there's not enough material. F. Scott Fitzgerald ("Wisdom Quotes," 2010b)

The family. We were a strange little band of characters trudging through life sharing diseases and toothpaste, coveting one another's desserts, hiding shampoo, borrowing money, locking each other out of our rooms, inflicting pain and kissing to heal it in the same instant, loving, laughing, defending, and trying to figure out the common thread that bound us all together. Erma Bombeck ("Conquering Stressful Family Hurdles," 2010)

Happiness is having a large, loving, caring, close-knit family in another city. George Burns ("Quote DB," 2010)

Family aches, wounds, struggles, and strife are the focus of this book – not because we are voyeuristic and enjoy looking at others' pain and suffering – but because, in varying degrees, all families experience darker moments. For some, the darkness is more a light shade of gray, while, for others, it is as dark as a moonless sky – and countless others are somewhere in between. We contend that all families, in fact, experience some darkness, and that darkness, as also acknowledged by Duck (1994), is an integral part of family life. Thereby, darkness within the family unit becomes a matter of gradation rather than an issue of presence or absence. This non-discriminatory nature of dark communicative dynamics begs further exploration because of its expansive impact on family functioning. Moreover, as Duck noted,

> when it is recognized that real lives are richly entwined with begrudging, vengeful, hostile, conflictive tensions and struggles, it will perhaps begin to be realized that one must also start to look at the ways in which people cope with them in life and then to theorize about them. (p. 6)

The fundamental goal of this book is to examine these struggles and to shed light on how such darkness is embedded in an interdependent system of individuals, dyads, family processes, and social institutions. Thus, this book focuses primarily on dark family interactions and is intended to supplement more general readings on family communication by advanced undergraduates, graduate students, and other professionals interested in this specific aspect of family life. It is important to note that, at times, we will explore theories or processes that may not necessarily be dark in and of themselves, but we find them illustrative of dark family life as well and, therefore, include them in our review. Moreover, our discussion of family communication processes will capture shades of darkness, ranging from tones of gray to hues that are clearly dark. We do so in order to capture the range of darkness that exists in family life. There are clearly some processes that are very dark, such as family incest or intimate partner violence, but there are also interaction patterns that are less dark, yet unhealthy nonetheless. Examples of these latter, grayer interaction patterns include parent–child conflict or the impact of narcissism on a family member's communicative abilities. Categorizing such a range of behaviors as dark may be controversial to some readers. However, as stated earlier, we believe it is important to recognize that family life is filled with happiness and strife, with struggles and joy. As such, we argue that to understand its fullness, family communication scholarship needs to capture such diversity in its theorizing. Again, we recognize that some may disagree with our categorization of particular behaviors as dark or with our co-mingling of black with gray interaction patterns. Some readers may be offended that we have classified particular behaviors as dark, while others may not. For readers at both of these extremes, we hope that you will read on with an open mind, knowing that our intention is not to offend but instead to provide a way of seeing family communication scholarship through a dark-colored lens.

Before beginning our discussion of the dark side of family communication, it is important to clarify several key terms that are the focus of this book – namely, what is family? What is family communication? And, finally, what is dark family communication? To answer these questions, we first will review various definitions of *family*, identifying the one definition that we will use to ground our discussion of family throughout the book. From there, we will articulate a definition of *family communication*, explaining various perspectives about communication embedded within the definition. The chapter concludes with discussion questions intended to generate further conversation about the material as well as an introduction to our fictional family, the Moores, whose experiences will help readers apply and process material presented in each of the subsequent chapters.

Key Definitions and Fundamental Assumptions

Family. As others have similarly observed (Baxter & Braithwaite, 2006b; Floyd, Mikkelson, & Judd, 2006; Vangelisti, 2004), defining the term family is almost as elusive as finding the pot of gold at the end of the rainbow. Just when you think you have it in sight, it slips out of your reach. Or, just as we think we have identified the best working definition of family, we encounter a family unit that is not captured by the definition. The reason for this, as described by Coontz (2000) and others (e.g., Floyd et al., 2006; Galvin, 2006) is that the American family is constantly evolving, and so too are our definitions. Table 1.1 presents a sampling of

Table 1.1. Examples of Definitions of Family Across Time

Murdock (1949)	"The family is a social group characterized by common residence, economic cooperation, and reproduction. It includes adults of both sexes, at least two of whom maintain a socially approved sexual relationship, and one or more children, own or adopted, of the sexually cohabiting adults" (p. 1).
Jorgenson (1989)	"A system of relations that comes about as individuals define those relations in their everyday communications with another" (p. 28).
Stacey (1990)	"A unit that may have residence but rather one that is based on "meaning and relationship" (p. 6).
Popenoe (1993)	"A relatively small domestic group of kin (or people in a kin-like relationship) consisting of at least one adult and one dependent person" (p. 529).
Bedford & Blieszner (1997)	"A family is a set of relationships determined by biology, adoption, marriage, and in some societies, social designation, and existing even in the absence of contact or affective involvement, and, in some cases, even after the death of certain members" (p. 526).
Allen, Fine, & Demo (2000)	"Characterized by two or more persons related by birth, adoption, marriage, or choice. Families are . . . defined by socioemotional ties, and enduring responsibilities, particularly in terms of one or more members' dependence on others for support and nurturance" (p. 1).
Koerner & Fitzpatrick (2002)	"A group of intimates who generate a sense of home and group identity and who experience a shared history and a shared future" (p. 71).
Sabourln (2003)	"The family is an agent of socialization, performing the tasks necessary to develop children and citizens" (p. 33).
Galvin, Bylund, & Brommel (2004)	"Networks of people who share their lives over long periods of time bound by ties of marriage, blood, or commitment, legal or otherwise, who consider themselves as family and who share a significant history and anticipated future of functioning in a family relationship" (p. 6).
Braithwaite & Baxter (2006)	"A social group of two or more persons, characterized by ongoing interdependence with long-term commitments that stem from blood, law, or affection" (p. 3).

definitions of family, revealing the diversity of how scholars have conceptualized this institution across time. The definitions range from a more traditional emphasis on heterosexual unions with "owned" or adopted children (Murdock, 1949) or on biological/legal kin (e.g., Popenoe, 1993) to a more post-modern stance based primarily upon intimacy (e.g., Turner & West, 2006/2002). More specifically, as noted by Fitzpatrick and Caughlin (2002), family definitions can be classified in three primary ways: (a) family structure definitions (how the family is comprised; e.g., Bedford & Blieszner, 1997); (b) psychosocial task definitions (functions of the family; e.g., functional view from Sabourin, 2003); and finally, (c) transactional process definitions (implies family's intimacy, loyalty, shared history, and group identity; e.g., Galvin, Bylund, & Brommel, 2004).

With so many different definitions of family, it may seem impossible to choose which one is "best." In our opinion, one definition is not necessarily better than the others per se (see Floyd et al., 2006, for a discussion of the pros and cons of different types of definitions). Instead, we agree with Sabourin (2003), who argues that it is not necessary to privilege one definition or one set of criteria over others when defining families, but, instead, "to be explicit about whatever criteria we use, both to subjects engaged in research and consumers of the written research product" (p. 41). Following this suggestion, we want to explicate our own stance toward family. In response to the current discourse, we assume a more post-modern, transactional approach toward family in this book, recognizing that in so doing we have constructed a particularly wide and more inclusive boundary around our conceptualization of family (see Floyd et al., 2006). More specifically, for our purposes we define family as *a social group of two or more persons, characterized by ongoing interdependence with long-term commitments that stem from blood, law, or affection*" (Braithwaite & Baxter, 2006, p. 3; see textbox below).

Thus, the definition of family we use in this text possesses fewer limitations than other current definitions of family. For instance, many scholars would argue that family members ought to be genetically tied. While our definition certainly allows for blood relation, we assert that families may also be bonded through legal obligations (e.g., family by marriage or through adoption) or by an intimate connection to another. Moreover, this definition causes one to examine complex relationships that, at first, might appear familial. Take the example of an adopted child who has never seen or spoken to her biological parents. Even though the child shares genes with her biological parents, she may or may not consider those individuals to be her family members. The approach to family that we assume in this book allows for both of those possibilities.

Furthermore, our definition of family is grounded in three assumptions: (1) families are systems, (2) families are coherent, and (3) families are constituted via social interaction (Vangelisti, 2004). These assumptions emphasize the idea that each member of the family affects and is affected by the others; therefore, each member's communication affects and is affected by the others'. As such, each of these assumptions foregrounds the role of communication in family formation and functioning.

Family: a social group of two or more persons, characterized by ongoing interdependence with long-term commitments that stem from blood, law, or affection. (Braithwaite & Baxter, 2006, p. 3)

Family Communication: messages that are intentionally or unintentionally exchanged both within a system of individuals who generate a sense of belonging and collective identity and who experience a shared history and future between these individuals and outsiders. (See Koerner & Fitzpatrick, 2002)

Dark Family Communication: synchronic or diachronic production of harmful, morally suspect, and/or socially unacceptable messages, observed and/or experienced at one or multiple interlocking structures of interaction, that are the products or causes of negative effects (temporary or long term) within the family system. (Baiocchi, Mbure, Wilson-Kratzer, Olson, & Symonds, 2009, p. 11)

Family Communication

With a definition of family in place, we now turn to defining family communication – a rather slippery construct to conceptualize because of its omnipresence in our lives. When something is so commonplace, it can be difficult to define. To complicate matters, scholarship tends to empirically examine the topic without offering a formal definition. Thus, definitions for family communication are not as bountiful as those for its fundamental component, family. However, several definitions can be found in key sources. For example, Le Poire (2006) proposed that family communication consists of messages sent intentionally, that are typically perceived as intentional, and that foster "shared meaning among individuals who are related biologically, legally, or through marriage-like commitments and who nurture and control each other" (p. 27). Additionally, Galvin et al. (2004) provided a "framework" for examining family communication that includes, in part, "the flow of patterned, meaningful messages within a network of evolving interdependent relationships located within a defined cultural context" (p. 49). While there are nuanced differences between these various definitions, they share one fundamental assumption: families are constructed and maintained via their communicative practices (Vangelisti, 2004). We share this basic premise and for our purposes, *family communication* is defined as *messages that are intentionally or unintentionally exchanged both within a system of individuals who generate a sense of belonging and collective identity and who experience a shared history and future, and between these individuals and outsiders* (see Koerner & Fitzpatrick, 2002; see the textbox above).

The two major elements of this definition deserve highlighting. First, it is important to remember that our communication with family can be planned and direct, or unplanned and without intention. Second, family communication occurs *within* the family system, but also occurs *between* the family system and others outside that system, such as family friends, neighbors, and colleagues. These two elements are especially salient as we discuss dark family communication.

Dark Family Communication

With clear definitions of family and family communication in place, we now turn to one more essential term to define, *dark family communication*. By its very nature, the dark side is "frequently hidden, secret, and therefore elusive" (Spitzberg & Cupach, 1994, p. 316), thereby making it difficult to define exactly what is the dark side of family. Spitzberg and Cupach (1994, 1998), the originators of the dark side metaphor in communication, identified "dark side" topics as those areas of study that often go unnoticed and/or unmentioned. However, they are also those things that are destructive, distortive, exploitive, objectifying, etc. (Spitzberg & Cupach, 1994, 1998). Nearly a decade later, the authors altered their definition, asserting that dark side communication could be viewed along two dimensions: morally/culturally acceptable (vs. unacceptable) and functionally productive (vs. destructive). Hence, one quadrant represented the "bright side" in which no "dark" existed (Spitzberg & Cupach, 2007). Concomitantly, Duck (1994) offered his own taxonomy of the dark side. He explained his perspective in a quadrant-like fashion as well, with a message sender's good or bad intentions running along one axis, and dark communication's inherent (trait-like) or emergent (state-like) nature running along the other. Notably, he addressed the idea of a positivity–negativity dialectic, claiming that relationships necessarily included both positive and negative aspects.

Building upon these authors' work, we consider dark family communication to be the *"synchronic or diachronic production of harmful, morally suspect, and/or socially unacceptable messages, observed and/or experienced at one or multiple interlocking structures of interaction, that are the products or causes of negative effects (temporary or long term) within the family system"* (Baiocchi et al., 2009, p. 11). To follow is a detailed description of four characteristics that are fundamental to our definition of dark family communication (see Table 1.2 for a summary).

Table 1.2. Characteristics of the Dark Side of Family Communication

Characteristics	Corresponding Assertions
The Nature of Dark Communication (The "What")	• Involves verbal and/or nonverbal messages that are deemed harmful, morally suspect, and/or socially unacceptable • Contains various shades of darkness in dark family communication • Contains a positivity and negativity dialectic
Meaning-Making Processes (The "How")	• Communication that is (in actuality or perceived as) intentional or unintentional • Experienced by interactants and/or observed by uninvolved individuals
Interlocking Interaction Structures (The "Where")	• Exists within and is influenced by four interlocking structures of interaction: individual, dyadic, familial, and social
Time (The "When")	• Involves effects that evolve over time (synchronic and diachronic) • Needs to be understood as both process and product

Characteristic 1: The Nature of Dark Communication

This first characteristic constitutes the "what" of our definition, or, more specifically, what comprises dark communication. In general, dark communication within the family is composed of communication processes and outcomes that involve the exchange of dark verbal and nonverbal messages. Verbal messages may include more *indirect* damaging messages (e.g., parental use of negative labels or double binds to discipline children, Stafford & Dainton, 1994) as well as *direct* messages such as verbal aggression or temper outbursts (Eriksen & Jensen, 2006). Nonverbal messages include but are not limited to the use of physical force such as spanking, physical abuse, and child maltreatment (Paolucci & Violato, 2004). Further, we define dark messages to be those that are "harmful, morally suspect, and socially unacceptable" (Baiocchi et al., 2009, p. 11). In sum, we assert that *dark family communication involves verbal and/or nonverbal messages that are deemed harmful, morally suspect, and/or socially unacceptable.*

Our definition of dark family communication also accounts for what we have entitled *shades of darkness.* Much existing scholarship on the dark side of communication often fails to account for the multidimensionality of darkness, instead casting it as a unidimensional construct. For example, relational conflict is often considered a dark topic alongside relational violence (for example, see Spitzberg & Cupach, 1998). Most would agree that conflict is typically less dark than relational violence. Yet, to date, no theoretical definition attempts to capture the nuances of these differences. These different forms of dark relational patterns are bound to vary in the types of messages produced and the impact those messages may have on the family system. It is imperative that these differences in the shades of darkness be accounted for when theorizing dark communication. Thus, we assert that *there are various shades of darkness in dark family communication.*

Next, it is important to acknowledge that not all dark communication within a family produces dark outcomes and neither does all bright family communication result in bright outcomes. The dynamics of family life and communication are much more complex than that, and our perspective on family darkness seeks to capture this complexity by acknowledging a positivity–negativity dialectic similar to one proposed by Duck (1994). So, for instance, a single mom and her daughter who have an established pattern of calling each other derogatory names during conflicts (dark communication behavior) may become so desensitized to this practice that they live a relatively satisfied family life overall (bright outcome). Or, a stepdad who excessively tells his daughter that she is the "best" (bright communication behavior) could unintentionally play a role in the girl's overly inflated sense of self and inability to handle adversity (dark outcome). These examples demonstrate how labeling processes and/or outcomes as dark can also involve confronting a dialectical tension between positivity and negativity. Furthermore, dysfunctional families can have moments of positive functionality, and vice versa – functional families can have dysfunctional moments. Our definition of dark family communication is intended to account for both of these centripetal and centrifugal forces and such a lens will be used to view the dark family communication literature. Therefore, we argue that *dark family communication contains a positivity and negativity dialectic.*

Characteristic 2: Meaning-Making Processes Involved with Dark Family Communication

Second, the darkness definition advanced here also seeks to draw our attention to the meaning-making processes that are both fundamental to communication interactions and integral to how darkness is defined, processed, and negotiated with family units. We see this component as the "how" of our definition – how the communicated messages are en/decoded with meaning. Two meaning-making processes are most central to our definition. As others have discussed, perspectives toward communication often assume a sender or receiver stance. This debate then leads to a discussion about the notion of intentionality – does a sender need to intentionally send a message in order for communication to have occurred and does a receiver need to intentionally receive a message? In the dark family context, the following scenario reflects this line of questioning. Let's say that Angela, a cousin to Jeffrey, sent an email message to multiple family members about the status of Aunt Betsy's health. Angela, however, did not include Jeffrey in the email distribution. Jeffrey subsequently learns of this through another cousin. Did communication occur between Angela and Jeffrey in this example? Some might say, "No, not if Angela did not intend to send the message to Jeffrey." Others would say, "Yes," because, regardless of intent, if Jeffrey received a message and assigned meaning to it (in this case, perhaps, a snubbing from cousin Angela), communication occurred. Even if a message was sent unintentionally, the fact that a message was "received" communicates meaning and, therefore, is an act of communication. Our approach to dark family communication accounts for both of these seemingly contradictory stances. We believe that dark family communication can be intentionally or unintentionally sent by an individual and can be assigned meaning by the interactants contrary to the meaning the sender intended. In other words, dark communication can occur both at the level of message construction (i.e., dark intent) and/or message deconstruction (i.e., dark meaning making). Thus, more formally noted, *dark family communication may be (in actuality or perceived as) intentional or unintentional.*

The discussion thus far focuses on the meaning making that occurs between the actual communicators. In other words, those who have "experienced" the communication. This is a common assumption embedded within the meaning-making deliberation – we typically assume that meaning making is capturing the processes involved with the direct interactants. However, as discussed by Spitzberg and Cupach (2007), there is a social (dis)approval dimension to the dark side. When we enter the dark side of communication, we walk through a door where not only the interactants themselves assign meaning to the actual communication events but additional uninvolved others assign meanings as well. This perspective is not isolated to dark interactions per se, but the fundamental essence of darkness involves making judgments about what may be harmful, morally suspect, or socially unacceptable – and those making such evaluations may not be the individuals directly involved. For example, a couple's heated discussion in a store may be normal to them but socially unacceptable to others standing close by. In this example, we have individual interactants assessing their communication one way, while observers evaluate it another way.

Whose interpretation is correct? The observer or the interactant? Dunbar and Burgoon (2005) also address this issue with regard to who is best qualified to report on acts of dominance – the participants or the observers? As these researchers note, there are arguments to be made for both sides. For instance, participants are best positioned to report the behavior because they are more "present" in the interaction than objective observers and more familiar with the nuanced behaviors of their partner. Conversely, a positivity bias has been found among participants relative to observers, suggesting participants are more likely to assign socially desirable meanings to the behaviors – especially to their own. Attribution theory (Heider, 1958; Weiner, 1986), and related concepts such as fundamental attribution error and the actor–observer bias help us understand this human tendency. According to Attribution theory, individuals have a need to make sense of their environment, and, in order to do so, attribute certain causes for particular behaviors. Individuals tend to attribute internal causes to their own positive outcomes, while attributing external causes to their negative outcomes (fundamental attribution error). On the other hand, individuals attribute another's negative outcomes to the other's behavior (actor–observer bias) as opposed to external forces. These tendencies are especially pronounced when the outcomes are negative, which is certainly the case during dark interactions.

Both sides of the actor–observer argument have merit. In fact, Dunbar and Burgoon (2005) assert that some level of concordance exists between the actor–observer ratings. Although a positivity bias may exist in the participants' self-ratings, it appears that there is a high correlation between the two parties' ratings. Yet, these researchers did find differences between the ratings of observers and participants, especially in regard to individual behaviors. It seems that the participants may have been more likely to use broader and more holistic judgments than attending to individual behaviors, when scrutinizing the actions involved. So, although there are commonalities between the parties' perceptions, there are also nuances to these interpretations that should not be ignored carte blanche. Thus, we believe it important to account for the perspectives of both the person(s) observing and the person(s) experiencing. There may be times when both parties' evaluations concur, but, when examining darker, dysfunctional interactions, an outsider's perspective is especially important to capture in order to move outside of the subjective box of the interactants themselves. As one might imagine, labeling one's behavior as harmful, socially unacceptable, or morally suspect may be too difficult to admit or too close to see, thereby increasing the need for a more arm's-length assessment. We feel that these are important issues to consider when theorizing dark communication and posit that *dark family communication may be experienced by interactants and/or observed by uninvolved individuals.*

Characteristic 3: Interlocking Interaction Structures

The dark family communication definition advanced in this chapter also accounts for different sites within the family "where" meaning making occurs – within the individual, within a dyad, within the family as a whole, and within society at large. It is instructive to think of these layers as interlocking interaction structures because they metaphorically capture different "locations" where communication takes place within families and where meaning making occurs. Admittedly, similar structures exist within all communication, and certainly, all families. However, such diversity of context is important to acknowledge when discussing the dark side due to its social and moral nature and, unfortunately, is often ignored in empirical examination of the topic.

First, with regard to the individual structure, we recognize that there are personality traits and characteristics that impact dark message construction and deconstruction (see Chapter 2 for more discussion). Communication is impacted by biological, cognitive, physical and psychological makeup, as well as characteristics related to gender, race and ethnicity, and socio-economic class. Psychologists, for example, have long attributed particular personality traits to behavioral consistencies, including extraverts' susceptibility to positive emoting (e.g., happiness), and neurotics' predisposition toward negative affect and anxiety-related behaviors (Eysenck & Eysenck, 1985; Larsen & Ketelaar, 1991; Plomin & Caspi, 1999; Zelinski & Larsen, 1999). These findings help explain why some individuals are more inclined to verbally or physically abuse. Hostile individuals (a destructive aggressive communication trait, according to Rancer and Avtgis, 2006), for instance, are likely to wish injurious and/or destructive consequences on another they dislike (Berkowitz, 1998). Chapter 2 will explore in more detail the scholarship on the role that individual personality and behavior play in dark family communication.

We also want to be sure to account for the dyadic nature of human relationships (Messman & Canary, 1998) and how such patterns influence dark side messages and outcomes. The *dyadic interaction structure* (reviewed in Chapter 3), specifically, allows us to examine dark communication processes and effects occurring at the structural level of typical pairs, such as the committed couple, parent–child, and sibling–sibling. For instance, communication patterns between parent and child have been shown to moderate the outcomes of corporal punishment (Barnett, Miller-Perrin, & Perrin, 2005). Research such as this confirms the need to incorporate the relational dynamics between dyads within the family into our understanding of dark family communication.

Similarly, the *family interaction structure* examines how family level processes can be dark or have dark outcomes (subject of Chapter 4). The influence of the family system in its entirety is evidenced clearly by the content, quality, and frequency of family interactions (Koerner & Fitzpatrick, 2002). For example, Schrodt (2009) found positive relationships between open family communication environments and family strengths and satisfaction. More specifically, the findings revealed that when families (particularly the parents) communicated in ways that encouraged open discussions, those environments could strengthen the family "by equipping family members with the information-processing and behavioral skills needed to cope with internal and external stress" (Schrodt, 2009, p. 181). In contrast, more closed, conformity- oriented environments were found to be inversely associated with family strengths and family satisfaction. It appears that family conformity negatively impacts a family's adaptability and flexibility during adversity as well as individual family members' levels of satisfaction.

Finally, our approach to dark family communication also considers how the *social interaction structure* (e.g., cultural context, the influence of religion and politics, the impact of the media, the historical time period, etc.) influences the messages produced, the effects of those messages, and the meaning assigned to the messages (Chapter 5 reviews these issues in more depth). For instance, in the United States during the early to mid nineteenth century, individuals may have been less likely to interpret certain racial epithets as hate messages and familial environments that prompted such speech as dark. However, in today's world, one would hope that more families (albeit not all, unfortunately) would judge this type of rhetoric as hateful – and thereby harmful, morally suspect, and socially unacceptable – or, in other words, dark.

Examining the overarching societal context also allows us to examine the issue of normalization (Barnett et al., 2005), or what may in other cultures be considered unacceptable and perhaps even illegal. Spanking, for instance, is more tolerated among African-American communities than European-American communities (Wilson & Morgan, 2004). Furthermore, examining the larger societal context allows us to examine the forces that may infiltrate and determine family interactions such as patriarchal gender relations and religion and spirituality (Barnett et al., 2005; Galvin, 2004). We approach culture as part of the larger societal context that influences the production, acceptance, and interpretation of dark messages. Although dark behaviors such as violence appear to characterize all human societies (Collins, 1981; Foucault 1976), there are cultural subtleties regarding, for instance, the level of acceptance and appropriate consequences for the victim and perpetrator. These subtleties may be influenced by other subcultures such as popular media culture of violence in the United States (Denzin, 1982; Weaver & Carter, 2006). For instance, Anderson and Dill (2000) found that exposure to violent video games has been associated with increased aggressive thoughts and behaviors in both the short term and long term. Exposure to certain types of media have also been found to produce changes in men's attitudes about aggression to women (Malamuth & Check, 1981, 1985). The dark messages and effects that can be observed in the interlocking structures are therefore influenced by culture and subcultures in society. Because these interaction structures provide a mechanism for understanding dark family communication, we assert that *dark family communication exists within and is influenced by four interlocking structures of interaction: individual, dyadic, familial, and social.* As noted, the structures form the basis for each of the subsequent chapters in this book and, therefore, will be discussed in more detail within each of those chapters.

Characteristic 4: Time

A final core characteristic of dark family communication, *time*, seeks to organize dark family communication, its interpretation, and its outcomes, both synchronically (one moment in time) and diachronically (occurring over time). Time allows us to capture the "when" of our conceptualization of family darkness. In their discussion of relational dialectics theory, Baxter and Braithwaite (2008) articulated this important time distinction as it relates to meaning making:

> Meanings do emerge in interactional moments, and in this sense, they are, at least momentarily, fixed and stable. But meaning is also fluid, which means that it is ultimately unfinalizable and "up for grabs" in the next interactional moment . . . meaning-making is envisioned as ongoing communicative work that results from the interanimation of different, often competing, discourses. (p. 353)

In other words, truly to understand darkness within families, we must acknowledge its dynamism, its fluidity. As a phenomenon, darkness is not static. Instead, its construction, enactment, meaning, and associated effects can vary within a moment and over many moments.

Within the scope of our definition then, synchronic and diachronic time distinctions aid us in understanding how the meaning individuals assign to dark family communication is not only produced, but also reproduced. For example, a mother and fifteen-year-old daughter may have a very serious conflict over the daughter's desire to go to an out-of-town concert with her friends. Very hostile words are exchanged (dark communication), eventually leading to the daughter running off to her bedroom and slamming the door on the way (short-term dark effect). After a few days of silence (longer-term dark communication and effect), the two of them slowly begin to talk again – but only about superficial daily musings, not about what happened a couple of days ago (continued dark and more diachronic communication). Both of them admit several years later, however, that this argument was a turning point in their relationship. With this outcome, we see both diachronic and synchronic effects of time on family communicative interactions.

A second function of time in our definition captures how dark messages, meanings, and effects evolve along with historical, social changes. Consider how a son's coming out to his parents might be met with a very different response if the conversation occurred in 1952 rather than 2012. Although same-sex romantic relationships are still not fully accepted in today's society, the social climate of the 1950s was much more unaccepting and thus would most likely have an impact on the parents' response to their son. This is just one example of how our definition of dark family communication seeks to capture such time-oriented realities of family life. More formally, we argue that *dark message production, meaning-making processes, and effects of these evolve over time (synchronic and diachronic)*. Furthermore, *dark family communication cannot be fully understood as either process or product; it must entail both* (see Table 1.1).

Chapter Summary

One thing all humans have in common is we come from some form of family. As we learned in this chapter, family can mean many different things to different people. No longer is the term only meant to reflect those relationships formed via blood or law. Instead, concepts such as closeness, interdependence, and intimacy capture more of the essence of the modern-day version of family. For us, family represents both those relationships formed by blood or law AND by affection and closeness. Unfortunately, that affection and closeness can include moments of disdain and distance and those ties that bind can sometimes feel more like a tightening noose. That complexity of dark and bright, happiness and sadness, functionality and dysfunction are the focus of this book. All families contain dark moments – some more severe, more impactful, and longer lasting than others. This book is intended to shed light on some of the more "hidden" areas of familial communication. More specifically, Chapter 2 reviews the impact of the individual on dark message construction and deconstruction. The topic shifts to an in-depth examination of dyadic types of dark family communication and processes in Chapter 3. The family, as a unit, is the focus of Chapter 4 as we explore dark sides of family level functioning. In Chapter 5, we broaden the discussion of dark family life to the role of culture, religion/politics, media, and historical time period. Finally, in Chapter 6, we close the book with an analysis of what the future holds for dark side of family communication scholarship, including a description of our Darkness Model of Family Communication and an explanation for how it could be one heuristic device for theorizing about this topic in the future. Along the way, you will be given a chance to apply each chapter's information to our fictional family, the Moores, whom you can meet in our introduction to the family (see the textbox below).

Meet the Moores

As you walk your dog down the street, you can't help but notice the outside of the Moores' home. The house and yard are almost picturesque: a perfect bay window in the living room that faces the street, the pristine white picket fence, and the freshly manicured lawn. But behind the picture-perfect example of the house and yard resides a family that is troubled and has its own secrets.

Meet Frederick (Fred) Moore: father/husband. A hard-nosed businessman in mergers and acquisitions. Fred is the son of an Air Force officer and stay-at-home mom, who was taught strict discipline from a very young age. As Fred progressed through school, his father traveled periodically and ran his house like an Air Force platoon, insisting his children be taught strict discipline and be successful. Failure was not an option. Today Fred is a strict disciplinarian.

Janice Moore: wife/mother. Janice grew up in an affluent suburb of Washington, DC. The third of four children, Janice spent most of her childhood and young adulthood trying to escape her older brother and sister's shadows. Later, the death of her sister splintered her family even more, casting Janice deeper into the shadows. Wanting to feel loved and cherished, Janice met Fred and married him six weeks later. Today, Janice is a stay-at-home mom, who hides the pain of not feeling love and acceptance.

Frederick (Freddie) Moore, Jr: oldest son. Freddie bears the brunt of his father's strict discipline and harsh ways. The oldest of three siblings, Fred is a junior in high school who enjoys spending time away from home, participating in activities such as marching band, baseball, and Honor Society. In his spare time, he draws comics and caricatures, hoping one day to escape his father's dream of Freddie joining the military.

Lucy Moore: daughter. Lucy is thirteen and in middle school. Lucy spends her free time designing clothes, lusting after the latest pop singer, and debating American Idol contestants with her friends. She also is active in her church youth group.

Robert "Bobby" Moore: youngest child. A seven-year-old with a daring imagination, Bobby is seen as the son Fred Moore never wanted but Janice dotes on. While interested in trains, Star Wars, and NASCAR, Bobby wants to be a crab fisherman on the Bering Strait when he grows up.

Gertrude Westley – aka "Grandma Trudy." After ending her dancing career, Trudy met her husband (of 37 years), Thomas, who was an Advertising Executive for a large Midwest advertising firm. She spent her life as a stay-at-home mom, doting on her two older children. After the death of her husband, she moved in with Janice's family because she could no longer financially support herself.

Steve Berry: friend of family. A junior in high school, who attends school with Freddie Jr. and participates in many of the same activities. He is the only child of a single working father, who works the graveyard shift four nights a week. Because of this, Steve spends many hours and nights at the Moore home and is considered a "member" of the family.

Discussion Questions

What characteristics and assertions from the definition of dark family communication are evidenced in the Moores' family scenario? What potential dark family communication issues are foreshadowed?

For Further Thought and Discussion

Theoretical Considerations

1. Review the definitions of family offered in Table 1.1 and consider the individuals you would deem as your "family members." How does your own conceptualization of your family change when each definition is applied?
2. What theoretical limitations exist, if any, to a transactional approach to family?
3. Your roommate turns to you and asks "What are you reading?" Your reply is "I am learning about dark communication," to which your puzzled room-mate says "What?" How do you explain dark communication?
4. Critique the characteristics of dark family communication advanced in this chapter. Are there any characteristics that you would change or delete? Can you think of other characteristics

that may be important to acknowledge in theorizing about the concept?

Practical Considerations

1. Imagine you are a family therapist. How might you use the characteristics of dark family communication to help a distressed family you are counseling?
2. Recall the last major conflict you had with a family member (or members). Apply each of the characteristics of dark family communication to the conflict and evaluate how each influenced the situation's outcomes.

Methodological Considerations

1. How might the characteristics of dark family communication be tested empirically?
2. How might a quantitative approach be used? What insights would be gleaned from testing the ideas using qualitative techniques? How might rhetorical or critical approaches be used?
3. What possible ethical challenges are involved in studying dark family communication?
4. What potential problems might arise when submitting a research proposal to a university's Human Subject Review Board to study dark family communication?

2

Individual Influence on the Darkness
of Family Communication

All too many of us can identify that one family member who is psychologically unstable or consistently causes problems, disrupts the family functioning, and communicates with others in unhealthy ways. This individual is the focus of Chapter 2. More precisely, as we learned in Chapter 1, the individual is one of four interaction structures to which we can turn our attention when examining dark family communication. As we will discuss, individuals can possess what could be considered dark personality traits or behavioral characteristics that influence how they construct and process family communication. Some individual dispositions can also change over time – an issue we explore at the end of the chapter. It is important to note that the systems approach to family makes it difficult to separate the individual from the other levels; however, our attempt to do so is mostly for illustration sake – to show how each component influences the system as a whole. Also important to note is the fact that our review is limited to individual psychological dispositions that have been shown to affect interpersonal and family interactions, particularly those which could be considered dark.

We begin the chapter by reviewing personality traits and how they impact individuals' behavior and communication. As the discussion will reveal, these characteristics are more trait-based. From there, we consider four types of social-personal dispositions that reveal how individuals' behaviors can be more state-based and, therefore, more impacted by and influential on the social environment. A section on relational dispositions follows in which we discuss the role of the individual in several relational processes (e.g., intimate violence and attachment patterns). A review of individually based communication patterns is presented before we draw the chapter to a close. At that point, you will learn more about the Moore family whom you were introduced to in Chapter 1 and be given an opportunity to engage in further discussion of the chapter material with our discussion questions.

Darkness and Individual Dispositions

While much of what is considered dark is socially constructed and interactionally created and maintained, we cannot ignore the fact that stable and enduring personality traits influence the communication of individual family members (e.g., Miller et al., 2000) and also influence and are influenced by the family environment (Nakao et al., 2000). Although defined in various ways, a relatively standard approach to personality sees it as "the complex set of unique psychological qualities that influence an individual's characteristic patterns of behavior across situations and over time" (Zimbardo, 1992, p. 509). A "dose" of certain characteristics will impact how an individual thinks, communicates, and behaves within the family unit (e.g., Botwin, Buss, & Shackleford, 1997). In fact, according to Duck (2011), "your personality affects your ability to connect and also the range of people with whom you can connect" (p. 56). Because of the extensive amount of research that has shown how a specific set of traits impact individuals and their interpersonal and familial worlds, we focus our attention on what is called the Big Five taxonomy of personality traits. Moreover, by their very nature of high and low ranges, the Big Five traits, as you will see, allow us insight into the positivity–negativity aspect of individual functioning from a dark perspective. In addition, we explore two additional maladaptive traits that have been shown to relate to communication.

Personality Defined

the complex set of unique psychological qualities that influence an individual's characteristic patterns of behavior across situations and over time (Zimbardo, 1992, p. 509)

Personality and Interaction: The Big Five

Personality psychology research empirically and theoretically espouses a five-factor model (FFM) of personality that is intended to be an exhaustive profile of the characteristic ways humans think, feel, and behave (see McCrae & Costa, 1999 for a review). The five dimensions are as follows: (a) Extraversion, (b) Agreeableness, (c) Conscientiousness, (d) Neuroticism, and (e) Openness. It is instructive to think of the Big Five factors as one large umbrella with corresponding sub-traits and behaviors (Ellis & Abrams, 2009). As explained in Table 2.1, each factor can be expressed on a continuum of high to low in each person. According to Ellis and Abrams (2009), individuals who are diagnosed with personality disorders are at the extreme end of the continuum for at least one factor. We expound on each factor of the FFM and its corresponding characteristics below. In particular, the discussion highlights how high and low levels of the personality factors might influence an individual's interactions and relationships with one or multiple members of the family.

Extraversion. Extraversion is known as the "dimension of personality in which an individual thrives on social interaction, likes to talk, takes charge easily, readily expresses opinions and feelings, likes to keep busy, has seemingly unending energy, and prefers stimulating environments" (Kail & Cavanaugh, 2007, p. 659). Said in a slightly different way, extraversion is often related to an individual's sociability. These are the type of family members who often enjoy the company of others and feel comfortable socializing and asserting themselves during family interactions (among others). In general, there is a large body of literature revealing the positive relationship between a person's extraversion and sociability (as compared to being introverted), including, for instance, extraverts' greater social skills, more agreeable behavior, higher levels of marital satisfaction, more friendships, and more adaptive parenting (for further information see Daly, 2002; La France, Heisel, & Beatty, 2004). Of particular interest to our topic here are the findings that show, for example, individuals how higher levels of extraversion tend to experience lower levels of parental stress (for a discussion see Vermaes, Janssens, Mullaart, Vinck, & Gerris, 2008) and, in conjunction with higher levels of agreeableness, conscientiousness, and openness and lower levels of neuroticism, found to engage in warmer behavior and to create consistent, more structured child-rearing environments (Prinzie, Stams, Dekovic, Reinjtjes, & Belsky, 2009). More specifically, in a study examining the stress of parents with children who have spina bifida, highly extraverted mothers in particular, reported lower levels of parental stress (Vermaes et al., 2008). Another study examining the relationship between family members' (parents and adolescents) perceived support and personality characteristics, Branje and colleagues (2004) found that highly extraverted parents were more likely to perceive higher levels of their own support giving and also to be perceived by their children as more support giving. Such robust findings led communication scholars Beatty, McCroskey, and Valenic (2001) to label extraversion as one of the three superfactors motivating all of communication.

So, as we have seen, extraversion is a trait that correlates with much positive, healthy, and "bright" communication behaviors – across contexts and certainly within families. Interestingly, however, we also know that individuals high in extraversion are not always engaging in *productive*, socially appropriate interactions. Extraversion, for instance, correlates highly with other traits such as dominance, forcefulness, bossiness (Lucas & Baird, 2004), impulsivity, narcissism, and self-defeating behaviors (Miller et al., 2009). Additionally, in a study examining parents in stepfamilies, Lee-Baggley, Preece, and DeLongis (2005) also discovered that partners high in extraversion reported using more negative marital conflict strategies, such as confrontation and interpersonal withdrawal. Interestingly, these individuals were likely to use more

Table 2.1. Big Five Personality Traits: Trait Range Characteristics and their Relation to Individual and Interpersonal Outcomes.*

Personality Trait	Characteristics of Low Range	Characteristics of High Range	Individual Outcomes	Interpersonal Outcomes
Extraversion	• Aloof • Uncomfortable in social settings • Laconic • Reserved • Quiet • Serious	• Outgoing • Attracted to social situations • Confident • Garrulous • Take charge • Readily express opinions and feelings • Like to keep busy	• Subjective well-being • Longevity, coping, resilience • Gratitude, inspiration • Depression (−) • Personality disorders (+/−)	• Peers' acceptance and friendship (children and adults) • Attractiveness • Status (adults) • Romantic relationship satisfaction • Adaptive parenting • Productive and appropriate interactions • Forcefulness, impulsivity, self-defeating • Marital instability
Openness	• Lacks curiosity • Is resistant to change • Conventional • Conservative • Unoriginal in thought • Rigid in approaches to diversity	• Vivid imagination • Intelligent, curious, and imaginative • Attracted to intellectual pursuits • Nonconforming and accepting of novel ideas	• Forgiveness • Inspiration • Substance abuse	• Marital instability • Marital satisfaction • Decreased relationship length
Agreeableness	• Uncooperative • Antagonistic	• Helpful to others • Trusting	• Gratitude, forgiveness, humor	• Peers' acceptance and friendship (children),

	• Cold, unfriendly, quarrelsome, hard-hearted, callous and egocentric • Disorganized • Aimless • Nonpersistent	• Cooperates in social settings • Accepting • Caring • Humor • Forgiveness • Warm • Sympathetic	• Longevity	• Cooperativeness, ability to control anger (in marriage) • Romantic relationship satisfaction • Marital stability • Conflict (−) • Perceived support within the family (+) • Antisocial behaviors (−)
Conscientious-ness	• Indolent • Readily surrenders to adversity • Unreliable • Frivolous • Irresponsible	• Persistent • Diligent • Scrupulous in interpersonal affairs • Task-efficient • Dependable	• Longevity • Risky health behaviors (−) • Substance abuse (−) • Personality disorders (+/−)	• Family satisfaction • Romantic relationship satisfaction • Relationship stability • Familial intergenerational relationships (−)
Neuroticism	• Calm • Readily recovers from trauma • Emotionally secure • Even-tempered • Self-content • Comfortable • Unemotional	• Emotionally labile • Prone to negative emotions • Easily traumatized • Anxious • Hostile • Self-pitying • Impulsive • Vulnerable	• Anxiety • Depression • Subjective well-being (−) • Humor (−) • Coping (−) • Personality Disorders (+/−)	• Family functioning (−) • Romantic relationship dissatisfaction • Conflict • Abuse • Marital dissolution • Affinity seeking • Adaptive parenting (−)

*Note: (−) indicates a negative relation between high levels of the trait and the outcome; (+/−) indicates a positive and a negative relation between high levels of the trait and the outcome.
Information from table adapted from Ellis & Abrams (2009); Kail & Cavanaugh (2007); Ozer & Benet-Martinez (2007); White, Hendrick, & Hendrick (2004).

relationship-centered behaviors when dealing with child misbehavior. Thus, family members who are extraverted may act in very positive ways, but they may also be forceful and self-centered.

We suspect most of us can think of someone in our family who might be classified as extraverted. Think of that person as you review Table 2.1 for a summary of all of the five factors and related individual and interpersonal outcomes. Contrastingly, you may know of family members who are low in extraversion, or introverted. These individuals are shy, quiet, and reserved. Thus, possessing low levels of extraversion, or introversion, also impacts communication with others in ways that contrast with what we learned about extraverts' interactional patterns above. Introverts tend to be withdrawn and primarily concerned with internal thoughts and processes (Ellis & Abrams, 2009). Low extraversion is also associated with depression and rejected peer status (for further review, see Ozer & Benet-Martinez, 2006). The introvert in your family may tend to shy away from social situations because he or she prefers to be alone (Costa & McCrae, 1988). For example, a study on shyness conducted by Duran and Kelly (1989) found that shy people tended to have fewer social experiences, more problems with articulation, and were less socially relaxed. These same researchers found that introversion also affected how a person interpreted what was said to him or her. Additionally, their research showed that these very shy individuals are harder on themselves than are others when evaluating how they handled an interaction. More specifically, Duran and Kelly (1989) found that although conversation partners did not perceive their shy counterparts as differentially competent, very shy people *perceived* they interacted poorly, lacked expression, and had partners who evaluated their communication skills negatively (Duran & Kelly, 1989). Thus, an introverted family member may be more likely to withdraw from interactions and to misinterpret communication. Less sociable behaviors and lower-level communication skills undoubtedly impact how this person communicates with others in the family, suggesting the potential for darker message processing and darker individual and family communication outcomes.

Interestingly, from an interactional standpoint, there is evidence to suggest that individuals with the same orientation toward sociability are more likely to have more successful interactions. Specifically, Cuperman and Ickes (2009) found that communication between two extraverts or two introverts yielded positive initial interactions, whereas conversations between one extravert and one introvert resulted in a poor initial interaction. This means that, in your family, two extraverts or two introverts are more likely to get along as compared to an extravert and an introvert, who are more likely to have negative interactions.

Openness. Do you know a family member who is open to new experiences, likes to try new things and is intelligent, curious and imaginative? If so, this person is considered high in openness (John & Srivastava, 1999; Kail & Cavanaugh, 2007; see Table 2.1). This person may also possess more positive virtues, as openness has been found to be related to such a belief structure (Thrash & Elliot, 2004). However, while an openness trait may be related to more positive behaviors, it (along with lower conscientiousness, which is discussed later) has also been found to be highly predictive of substance abuse disorders (Trull & Sher, 1994).

Conversely, family members scoring low in openness would be more likely to show narrow interests and shallowness (John & Srivastava, 1999) as well as be resistant to change and lack curiosity (Ellis & Abrams, 2009). Low openness may also be, according to Ozer and Benet-Martinez (2006), "the most important personality trait in terms of impact on identity development" (p. 408). This means that a family member who is less open to new experiences or lacks a curiosity about things may also have a corresponding identity. For example, one study (Clancy & Dollinger, 1993) found that individuals with low openness possessed what these researchers called a *foreclosure identity status* (i.e., one in which the individual blindly accepts the identity and values that others have for him/her, Marcia, 1980). Another study conducted by Benet-Martinez and Haritatos (2005) also explored the relationship between openness and identity (among other variables). This research is especially important for families consisting of bi-cultural individuals. Specifically, the researchers used the Bicultural Identity Integration (BII) framework as a way to test individual differences in bi-cultural identity negotiation. The framework is intended to capture to what degree "biculturals" integrate their mainstream and ethnic cultural identities. BII framework examines the extent to which these individuals' joint cultural identities are compatible and integrated as opposed to oppositional and difficult to integrate. In this study, the researchers focused on the bicultural experiences of first-generation Chinese Americans ($N = 133$) with the goal of trying to uncover individual differences (e.g., personality) in the BII process and related psychosocial antecedents. Results showed that openness (or the lack thereof) was especially important when it came to integration of bicultural identities. More specifically, the authors noted that

> individuals who are rigid and closed to new experiences are more likely to compartmentalize cultural identities, feel stressed about their linguistic abilities, support a separation acculturation strategy, and be less biculturally competent (all factors that, in turn, are important predictors of cultural distance and/or conflict). (Benet-Martinez & Haritatos, 2005, p. 1036)

Agreeableness. If others consider you to be very kind, affectionate, trusting, and helpful, you might score highly on the factor of agreeableness. Moreover, research has shown that humor (Cann & Calhoun, 2001), forgiveness (Thompson et al., 2005), and other healthy interpersonal processes, such as marital satisfaction, cooperativeness, and an ability to control anger during conflicts (for a review, see Daly, 2002) are associated with agreeableness. With regard to families with adolescents, Branje, van Lieshout, and van Aken (2004), found that agreeableness was the Big Five factor most strongly related to perceived support within the family. Agreeable individuals, then, are often warm and are able to express sympathy and empathy, while those scoring low on agreeableness might associate more with traits such as being cold, unfriendly, quarrelsome, and hard-hearted (John & Srivastava, 1999).

Studies often document a negative relationship between agreeableness and antisocial behaviors, such as risky sex and substance abuse (see Miller et al., 2009, for a review). According to Miller and colleagues (2009), low agreeableness (disagreeableness), along with extraversion are two of the major personality traits most strongly associated with narcissism (defined in a following section) (p. 787). Such a finding makes sense given that research suggests disagreeable individuals are also found to be callous and egocentric (Miller et al., 2009) and antagonistic and uncooperative (Ellis & Abrams, 2009). Furthermore, low agreeableness, when associated with its subcomponent hostility, has also been shown to predict poorer physical health, earlier mortality, sympathetic nervous system activation related to coronary artery disease, and peer rejection (Ozer & Benet-Martinez, 2006). Overall, as noted by Ozer and Benet-Martinez (2006), low "agreeableness (e.g., hostility) seems to be most directly associated with disease processes" (p. 406) and "negative relationship outcomes such as relationship dissatisfaction, conflict, abuse, and ultimately dissolution" (p. 410).

Conscientiousness. Conscientious individuals are organized and reliable. They are typically persons on whom one can depend, are task-efficient, and are more committed in close relationships (Ozer & Benet-Martinez, 2006). Conscientiousness has also been shown to predict longer lives. On the other hand, non- or low conscientious individuals seem to score higher on trait measures including carelessness, frivolity, and irresponsibility (John & Srivastava, 1999; Zimbardo, 1992). With such corresponding tendencies, it is not surprising then that individuals who are low in conscientiousness are also likely to experience more negative familial intergenerational relationships and engage in riskier health behaviors, such as smoking, unhealthy eating, not exercising (Ozer & Benet-Martinez, 2006), and abusing drugs (Trull & Sher, 1994).

Neuroticism. Perhaps one of the most widely known personality factors, neuroticism, correlates highly with a long list of traits, ranging from anxiety, moodiness, and irritability, to instability, temperamentalism, and self-pity. Therefore, traits such as stability, calmness, and contentedness reflect low neuroticism (see Table 2.1). In the realm of family functioning, Vollrath, Neyer, Ystrom, and Landolt (2010) suggested that a highly neurotic individual's tendency to have a critical, negative view of the world and him or herself also extended to the individual's ideas of family functioning. Specifically, in their study of the dyadic effects of parent personality on family functioning during the time a child was hospitalized, these researchers found (among other findings) that low neuroticism (and high conscientiousness) correlated with better family functioning. Conversely, mothers' neuroticism was negatively associated with their own perceptions of family functioning, underscoring the "overwhelming influence of a person's own personality on his or her relationship experiences" (p. 36).

In general, neuroticism has been found to correlate inversely with affinity seeking, or people's ability to get others to like them and see them in a positive light (Heisel, La France, & Beatty, 2003), with expressing emotion (Riggio & Riggio, 2002) and to correlate positively with negative relational outcomes, such as marital dissolution (Cramer, 1993; Rogge, Bradbury, Hahlweg, Engle, & Thurmaier, 2006); less adaptive parenting; more complaining; and more negativity (for further information, see Daly, 2002; Ozer & Benet-Martinez, 2006).

Two additional maladaptive personality traits and their relation to dark interactions

Narcissism. Narcissists have "positive and inflated self views, related to uniqueness, superiority, entitlement and authority ... They have a tendency to boast about their achievements, and, in general, have an arrogant attitude about their abilities" (Konrath, Bushman, & Grove, 2009, p. 1199). Narcissistic individuals tend to inflate themselves to acquire more attention at the expense of others; that is, they show a lack of respect for others by focusing on their own feelings (Asada, Lee, Levine, & Ferrara, 2004). They also externalize failure by becoming angry and blaming others (Rhodewalt & Morf, 1998), find attractive those people who show them admiration (Campbell, 1999), and have unstable self-esteem and mood variability and intensity on a daily basis (Rhodewalt, Madrian, & Cheney, 1998). Interestingly, Asada and colleagues (2004) found that narcissistic people use empathy in a reverse order: For example, most people consider the perspective of others before reacting in a situation. However, narcissistic people react first in order to preserve their self-image, and then consider the other conversational partner's perspective. Such behavior seems to exist within families as well. For example, Greenberg and Mitchell (1983) found that narcissistic parents were less likely to take another's perspective and looked to their children to fulfill their own needs for admiration. Ehrenberg, Hunter, and Elterman (1996) also found that narcissistic divorced parents were less likely to make childcare decisions based upon their children's needs. Instead, they tended to stick to their own ideas rather than work cooperatively with their ex-partner for the good of the children.

All of these studies shed light on how narcissists communicate. "Conversational narcissism" is thought to exist when someone is extremely self-focused during conversations without concerning him or herself with the cares of others (Vangelisti, Knapp, & Daly, 1990). Communication strategies used by narcissistic people include boasting, asking questions to feel superior on a topic, using one-up statements, shifting the focus of discussion to themselves, and showing impatience when others speak (Vangelisti et al., 1990). Furthermore, narcissists are sensitive to both positive and negative feedback and react more extremely to both, as compared to non-narcissistic people (Rhodewalt et al., 1998). Not surprisingly, Vangelisti and colleagues (1990) found that narcissistic people are rated as less socially attractive than those who are not boastful.

Machiavellianism. Machiavellianism is defined as a tendency for some people "to manipulate or deceive others for advantage or gain. The results are the goal of the Machiavellian person; the means by which one achieves the results are only important insofar as they affect the results" (Ellis & Abrams, 2009, p. 610).

Machiavellianism was named after Niccolò Machiavelli, an early sixteenth-century diplomat and political figure, who advised people that they could become powerful leaders if they encountered a little luck (called *fortuna* in Italian) and were willing to be assertive, fearless, and self-confident (known in Italian as *virtù*) (Ellis & Abrams, 2009). The general philosophy of Machiavellian individuals – or, "Machs" – is to get their way, or "win," at all costs. Therefore, Machs tend to be manipulative, cunning, and insincere; they exploit others and are considered unethical (Christie & Geis, 1970). Machiavellianism has also been found to correlate negatively with prosocial behavior and love for family (McHoskey, 1999) and to relate positively to hyper-competitiveness (Stewart & Stewart, 2006). In a study on interpersonal influence, people high in Machiavellianism tended to use indirect tactics, most prominently deceit (Grams & Rogers, 1989). In an older study, Kraut and Price (1976) examined the relationship between parent and child Machiavellianism, finding that high Mach parental scores positively corresponded with their children's ability to deceive others successfully. Again, those predisposed to Machiavellianism express these manipulative tendencies through more anti-social communication behaviors.

In sum, this section has revealed how individuals can possess certain personalities that influence their behavior and communication. It is important to recognize that, even though we reviewed the traits separately, they actually work in concert with each other to form overall personality profiles and behavioral patterns. One such example can be found in a study on the relationships among narcissism, impulsivity, and self-defeating behaviors conducted by Miller and colleagues (2009). These researchers found, in part, that narcissism and impulsivity predicted aggression, and high extraversion and low agreeableness mediated the relationship between narcissism and self-defeating behaviors. In addition to underscoring the complex nature of personality, we assert that these personality traits can influence both how someone constructs a message and how an individual is affected by a message – ideas grounded in our theoretical orientation toward dark family communication. For example, it is conceivable that an introverted young gay male might "construct" a socially awkward message when trying to sense whether his family is open to him disclosing his sexual orientation. Or, the introverted man may be so aloof that he is less likely to deconstruct a message accurately, perhaps leaving him unaware that his sister is aware of his sexuality and, in turn, assigning meaning to the apparent lack of communication as "they just don't want to know." This is one example of how personality, a trait-based phenomenon, is a part of dark family communication. Another way of viewing the role of the individual in such family functioning is to look at more *state-based* individual patterns that are especially context-dependent. We turn to a discussion of these social-personal dispositions next.

Darkness and Social-Personal Dispositions

Depression. It has been said that more human suffering can be attributed to depression than any other disease affecting humankind (see Beck & Alford, 2009). According to the World Heath Organization (2010) "depression is a common mental disorder that presents with depressed mood, loss of interest or pleasure, feelings of guilt or low self-worth, disturbed sleep or appetite, low energy, and poor concentration" ("What is Depression?"). The literature on depression is vast and beyond the scope of our chapter. One aspect of it that is especially relevant to our discussion here, however, is the intersectionality of depression and interpersonal/familial interactions. There is a strong association between depression and loneliness, poor social skills, interpersonal rejection, relational distress, and family dysfunction (abuse/neglect) (for further review, see Segrin, 2001). More specifically, marriages in which one spouse is considered depressed, for example, are labeled as more hostile and less friendly (McCabe & Gotlib, 1993). Depression does not just impact the depressed spouse, it impacts them as both a partner and a parent. For instance, Segrin, Badger, Meek, Lopez, Bonham, and Sieger (2005) found that as breast cancer patients' emotional well-being (including levels of depression) improved or deteriorated so did their partners'.

We also know that there are important gender dynamics involved in depression, revealing the potential for dark power dynamics and their effects. Women are more likely to exhibit depression than men (Nolen-Hoeksema, 1987) and differ from men in how they care for their depressed male partners (Duggan, 2007). The study by Duggan explored actions taken by the non-depressed partner and found that male partners of depressed women tended to label their partner's depression as problematic and then helped them to get well. Over time, the men decreased their attempts at helping their partner, which tended to further exacerbate their partner's depressive behaviors. Conversely, female partners tended to help their depressed male partners get well *before* labeling their depression as problematic. Women also tended to change their strategies and eventually reverted to helping their partner while simultaneously reinforcing the depressive behaviors.

Substance abuse disorder. According to the US Department of Health and Human Services (2008), "addiction is a chronic, often relapsing brain disease that causes compulsive drug seeking and use despite harmful consequences to the individual who is addicted and to those around them" (p. 1). One's substance abuse or substance dependence not only has major effects on the individual, but also on the welfare of others and society (American Psychiatric Association, 2000), particularly one's family (Hudak, Krestan, & Bepko, 2005; Jackson, 1954/2002). Once again, the literature on substance abuse is much broader than we can account for in this section. However, with regard to its relation to dark family communication, studies have found many negative effects on family functioning. For instance, parental alcoholism has been found to be negatively associated with adult child self-esteem and parental disregard (Rangarajan & Kelly, 2006), and positively associated with violent and abusive behaviors (Lease, 2002; Leonard & Senchak, 1996).

A key theory on substance abuse that is grounded in communication and that has now been extended to include eating disorders, gambling, and other types of addiction is Le Poire's (1992, 1994; for a review see Le Poire, 2004) Inconsistent Nurturing as Control (INC) Theory. This theoretical framework clearly articulates how a dark issue at an individual level can also affect the relationship levels. The theory explicates the paradoxes involved when one *functional partner* inconsistently nurtures or punishes the *afflicted partner* for his/her behavior (Prescott & Le Poire, 2002). In general, according to Prescott and Le Poire (2002), "INC theory argues that the functional partners of afflicted individuals have competing goals to simultaneously nurture and control their afflicted partner while attempting to diminish an undesirable behavior" (p. 64).

While most would assume the functional partner to have control in the relationship, Duggan, Dailey, and Le Poire (2008) assert that it is the afflicted partner who actually has the control because the functional partner's actions are dependent on the afflicted partner's. Furthermore, after a particularly bad night of substance abuse, the functional partner may care for the afflicted partner. The abuser feels indebted to the stable partner and returns to those behaviors out of guilt. Thus, the stable partner unwittingly helps to perpetuate the abusive behaviors. Le Poire, Hallett, and Erlandson (2000) discovered that successful partnerships were those in which the stable partner consistently punished abusive behavior and reinforced alternative behaviors. In general, this theory illustrates how one individual's problem with abusing substances is transposed onto others: an entire family can feel the effects of another's alcohol abuse.

Self-injury. Hurting oneself is another dark form of individual behavior that impacts families. The most common method of self-injury is cutting the body, using a knife or razor, usually on the arms, legs, and stomach (Nock & Prinstein, 2004). Other less common methods of self-injury include scratching the skin until it bleeds, forcing objects under the skin, or burning the skin. We have learned that self-injury occurs as a means of self-soothing or seeking help (Klonsky, 2009). Nock (2010) noted that those who cause injury to themselves may possess both intrapersonal and interpersonal vulnerability factors that affect their ability to handle stressful and aversive events. Interestingly, a study conducted by Levesque and colleagues (Levesque, Lafontaine, Bureau,

Cloutier, & Dandurand, 2010), relating self-injury to romantic attachment styles (discussed below) and partner violence, found that both men and women experience non-suicidal self-injury (NSSI) thoughts when they experience anxiety over abandonment. More specifically, the researchers found that adults with anxiety prone attachment styles were more likely to use NSSI behaviors as compared to adults with secure attachment styles who were more likely to adapt to and work through their emotional states. Finally, the study also found that violence in romantic relationships was another predictor of NSSI behaviors for men and women (Levesque et al., 2010). Thus, it seems that adults who cannot regulate their emotions may redirect violence on to themselves.

Eating disorders. According to the National Institute of Mental Health (NIMH, 2007), an eating disorder (ED) is "present when a person experiences severe disturbances in eating behavior, such as extreme reduction of food intake or extreme overeating, or feelings of extreme distress or concern about body weight or shape" (p. 2). With regard to basic demographics, evidence shows that EDs tend to appear first in adolescence but can also develop in later life and that women and girls develop EDs at much higher rates than men and boys. In addition, there are common forms of eating disorders – anorexia nervosa and bulimia nervosa. Anorexia nervosa is "characterized by emaciation, a relentless pursuit of thinness and unwillingness to maintain a normal or healthy weight, a distortion of body image and intense fear of gaining weight, a lack of menstruation among girls and women, and extremely disturbed eating behavior" (NIMH, 2007, p. 5). In contrast, according to the NIMH, frequently consuming large amounts of food and feeling out of control or over-eating characterizes bulimia; the binge-eating is then followed by some form of purging, be it vomiting, fasting, excessive exercising, or consuming laxatives or diuretics. The binging–purging cycle usually happens several times per week.

Despite significant amounts of research conducted on the topic, many of the underlying causes remain elusive (NIMH, 2007). With that said, however, several factors have been associated with the presence of eating disorders. In general, as noted by Prescott and Le Poire (2002), there are four main categories of risk: psychological, socio-cultural, biological, and familial. According to Leslie and Southward (2009), in the early stages of understanding the root cause of ED behavior, the family, and particularly the mother, was believed to play a central role. More specifically, enmeshed or disengaged parent–child relationships and poor family communication were thought to be the cause. However, feminist family therapists critiqued the excessive parent and mother blaming that was happening in both scholarship and therapeutic interventions, arguing that such an approach was too narrow. These voices helped expand our understanding of the root causes and significant correlations of ED. For one, experts in this area began to look at society's role. In our culture, being thin is highly valued, especially in the media, which may distort the body image of people, contributing to their development of an eating disorder. Thus, we have come to recognize that society *and* family culture focused on the thin ideal can impact the development of ED. Taking this mediated image one step further, researchers are now examining to what degree ED may be a coping strategy for oppressed individuals (especially women and minorities). In the words of Leslie and Southward (2009),

> Young women are taught by both their families and the larger culture that success, intimacy, and security are intricately linked to the perceived levels of attractiveness and, particularly for White women, thinness. . . . From this, it has been posited that the oppressive nature of these expectations may manifest through EDs, in which self-starvation and purging are nonassertive, yet powerful, ways in which women resist their socially prescribed roles. (p. 336)

While spotlighting the behavior of the individual, the social–personal dispositions reviewed highlight how such behaviors cannot be separated from the context and culture in which they are embedded. Most notably, these dark issues such as depression or eating disorders influence how a person communicates and how the family communicates with that person. The bi-directionality of the individual–family influence on communication processes cannot be emphasized enough. For instance, an alcoholic stepfather may use aggression when communicating with his stepson; in turn, the son may become disengaged and eventually engage in self-defeating behaviors. Such negative actions by the son prompt the father to confront him, but the father does so in a hostile way, setting in motion a whole new disengaging-engaging/hostility–silence cycle. The relational aspect of this scenario is the focus of the next section, which examines the specific association between individual behavior and dark relational dynamics.

Darkness and Relational Dispositions

There are a variety of concepts and processes that scholars have examined in order to understand how individuals relate to others – and, more specifically, how characteristics and traits of the individual influence their relating. The possibilities are endless, and it is beyond the scope of this book to address them all. Instead, we focus on two individually based relational processes that are either dark by nature or provide insight into dark individual behavior in a relational context. These processes include relational attachment and violence-oriented individuals.

Individual and relational attachment. Perhaps one of the most prolific lines of family scholarship is that related to attachment (for a review, see Mercer, 2006) and attachment theory. Countless books, chapters, and journal articles have given us insight into the role that attachment plays in how children, and later adults, form bonds with others and live healthy, productive lives. Unfortunately, we cannot do justice to the amount of scholarship on the attachment theory and corresponding styles. Yet, we would be remiss if we did not review their basic components and relevant findings associated with the dark side of family life, which is what we present next.

Created to explain the developmental bonds that infants create with their caregivers (Ainsworth, 1969), attachment theory is grounded in "the propensity of human beings to make strong affectional bonds to particular others" (Bowlby, 1977, p. 201). Children form their primary attachment style at a young age with their primary caregiver. A secure base is developed when an infant perceives that the caregiver is responsive and available; conversely, insecure attachments develop when a child perceives his/her caregiver to be inadequately responsive (Bowlby, 1969/1982, 1973; Kirkpatrick & Hazan, 1994).

Over time, according to Kirkpatrick and Hazan (1994), "individual differences in the functioning of the system emerge based on the infant's expectations of caregiver responsiveness and dependability" (p. 123). Bowlby (1973) asserted that, although there may be some modification during childhood, these expectations are formed mostly by age five and persist relatively unchanged throughout one's lifetime, thereby following individuals from cradle to grave (Bowlby, 1979). The reason for this continuity is because the expectations come to serve as internal working models, or cognitive representations, of how the child (and later the adult) views him/herself, others, and relationships (Ainsworth, Blehar, Waters, & Wall, 1978; Bowlby, 1973; Kirkpatrick & Hazan, 1994). The working models are grounded in attitudes, expectations, and beliefs about *self* (whether one is worthy of love and support), *others* (whether others are viewed as trustworthy and dependable), and the relation between the two (Horppu & Ikonen-Varila, 2001). Thus, because of the stability and cross-age continuity (Collins & Read, 1990) of the working models, they play an important role in understanding the impact that early childhood relationships have on future adult bonds. Attachments formed in childhood become adults' characteristic style for attaching to others throughout their life, thereby influencing their expectations and perceptions of adults' social world and relational behavior, which, in turn, leads them to behave in ways that are in accordance with their mental models of self and other (Ainsworth, et al., 1978; Becker, Billings, Eveleth, & Gilbert, 1997; Bowlby, 1977, 1980; Collins & Read, 1990; Guerrero, 1996).

The first empirical testing of Bowlby's theory was conducted by Ainsworth and colleagues (1978), who identified three distinct parent–child attachment patterns: secure, ambivalent, and avoidant. Because their studies supported Bowlby's stability hypothesis that the attachment patterns formed in childhood became rather fixed, a trait-like perspective toward attachment patterns was established. The individual difference approach was extended by Hazan and Shaver (1987), whose work was some of the first to apply attachment theory to adult romantic relationships paralleling Ainsworth et al.'s three-category parent–child model. The labels assigned to the adult attachment styles included secure, avoidant, and anxious/ambivalent. Bartholomew and Horowitz (1991) later expanded Hazan and Shaver's typology to four (secure, dismissive, preoccupied, and fearful avoidant) by combining the two dimensions of the working model – view of self (positive and negative) and view of others (positive and negative). In general, people who possess a positive model of self see themselves as worthy of love and support and those with a positive model of others view them as trustworthy, available, and caring (Horppu & Ikonen-Varila, 2001).

Researchers have identified numerous *individual* based outcomes associated with attachment styles. Perhaps not surprisingly, secure attachments tend to correlate with more positive psychological states and behavioral patterns, while the opposite is true of insecure (anxious/ambivalent, fearful, avoidant, dismissing) styles. For example, with regard to personality, Becker and colleagues (1997) found that secure attachments were positively correlated and fearful attachments were negatively correlated with all of the Big Five personality traits. The preoccupied style also corresponded with all of the traits with the exception of agreeableness. Individuals with secure attachments also report higher levels of self-esteem and self-confidence as well as lower scores on self-conscious anxiety and unfulfilled hopes than do people with insecure attachments (Feeney & Noller, 1990).

Individuals' experiences with and regulation of affective states also appear to differ by attachment styles. For example, compared to secure styles, insecure attachments have been found to associate positively with loneliness (Hazan & Shaver, 1987; Kobak & Sceery, 1988), anxiety (Mikulincer & Orbach, 1995), stronger fears of death at a lower level of awareness (Mikulincer, Florian, & Tolmacz, 1990), peer ratings on low ego-resiliency and high hostility, anxiety, and personal distress (Kobak & Sceery, 1988), and the inability to repress negative emotions and inhibit emotional spreading (Mikulincer & Orbach, 1995).

Further, Bartholomew and Horowitz (1991) discovered that different insecure attachment styles were associated with various interpersonal problems. For example, dismissing styles were associated with being hostile and cold. Fearfuls were reported to be overly passive. In contrast, preoccupied individuals were overly expressive to the point of being dominating.

Finally, perhaps the most often examined area in adult attachment research is how love relationships are experienced by individuals with different romantic attachment styles. Consistent evidence shows that individuals with secure attachments experience love as happy, friendly, and trusting (Feeney & Noller, 1990, 1991; Hazan & Shaver, 1987) and report higher levels of intimacy, passion, and commitment (Levy & Davis, 1988). In contrast, love of an avoidant adult is characterized by a fear of closeness and intimacy as well as a lack of trust (Feeney & Noller, 1990; Hazan & Shaver, 1987) and low levels of intimacy, viability, commitment, and satisfaction (Levy & Davis, 1988). This was especially true of avoidant men in a study conducted by Kirkpatrick and Davis (1994), who found that these men were less committed, satisfied, intimate, and caring than secure men, and less committed and passionate than anxious men. Both avoidant men and women in this analysis reported lower levels of relationship viability than their secure counterparts. Additionally, avoidants are more likely than other styles to report never having been in love (Feeney & Noller, 1990). On a related note, they are also more pessimistic about real love, believing it rarely happens. If it does happen, however, they believe that it rarely lasts (Hazan & Shaver, 1987). When they do encounter love, individuals with avoidant attachments tend to feel either low levels of emotional intensity (Feeney & Noller, 1991) or emotional highs and lows (Hazan & Shaver, 1987) and to experience relationship break-up more often than the other types (Feeney & Noller, 1992).

Violence-oriented individuals and relationships. Numerous frameworks have been used in an attempt to explain family violence, including, just to name a few, a psychological lens (Dutton & Bodnarchuck, 2005), a communication skills deficiency model (Infante, Chandler, & Rudd, 1989), a relational-control based typology (Olson, 2004), a sociological approach (Johnson, 2008; Loseke, 2005), and a feminist perspective (Yllo, 2005). Within the communication discipline, approaches to the study of family violence are equally diverse. In his 2009 survey of the field, Cahn identified three primary approaches used by communication scholars to "communicatively" study family violence: (a) a communicator personality trait approach, (b) a communication cognition approach, and (c) a communication interaction approach. We encourage those interested in learning about these multiple approaches to investigate the various sources listed. Our focus here, however, will be primarily on the psychological aspect of battering and abuse, given this chapter's examination of the individual's role in the dark side of family communication.

According to Dutton and Bodnarchuk (2005), a robust finding in the violence research is the positive correlation between personality disorders and assaultive populations. For example, as compared to 15 to 20 percent of the general population, 80 to 90 percent of court- and self-referred wife assaulters have personality disorders. Such disorders have been used to differentiate types of batterers from one another, resulting in various categories and typologies. Gottman and colleagues' Type 1 (antisocial) and Type 2 (impulsive) batterers is one such typology (Gottman et al., 1995). These researchers conducted a study with a group of severely violent male batterers, measuring their psychophysical responses during lab-based conflicts with their partners. Interestingly, the Type 1, antisocial batterers' heart rates *decreased* during the conflicts, whereas the heart rates increased during the conflicts for the impulsive Type 2 batterers. As compared to Type 2 men, Type 1 batterers were also more likely to be generally violent (aggression extending beyond the marriage), to have witnessed aggression as a child, and to exhibit antisocial and aggressive-sadist tendencies.

A tripartite typology of male batterers was proposed by Holtzworth-Munroe and Stuart (1994) after a thorough review of existing typologies. According to the researchers, three dimensions had been used in past work to distinguish different types of batterers: (a) the severity and frequency of physical, sexual, and psychological violence; (b) the degree to which the violence was contained within the family or extrafamilial (referred to as "generality" of violence); and (c) the male's psychopathology or personality disorders. They used these dimensions to hypothesize about the profiles of three different types of batterers. First, the authors estimated that "dysphoric/borderline batterers" comprise approximately 25 percent of treatment samples, are impulsive, and confine their moderate to severe levels of violence to their family; they are also emotionally volatile, psychologically distressed, depressed, and substance abusers. Second, "generally violent/antisocial batterers" are believed to make up 25 percent of all batterers and are more likely, when compared to the other men, to engage in violence outside the home. These batterers also are expected to show signs of an antisocial personality disorder and exhibited drug/alcohol addiction. Finally, the "family-only batterers," as the name implies, are theorized to confine their violence to the family, to enact less severe forms of aggression, and to be the least likely of the types to engage in sexual and psychological abuse. The researchers also predicted that this group would make up at least 50 percent of community and treatment-based batterer samples. In a follow-up study testing this typology, Holtzworth-Munroe and colleagues (2000) sampled 102 maritally violent men (among others) and found support for the three sub-types identified in the 1994 review. Their analysis also yielded a fourth sub-type, which was labeled "low level antisocial" and whose profile seemed to fit best between the family-only batterers and the generally violent/antisocial batterers.

In brief, this section has examined individuals' relational behavior, particularly dark tendencies. As we have discussed, some people may enact darker forms of familial behavior due to attachment patterns formed in early childhood or because of some maladaptive personality traits or tendencies. In addition to these aforementioned dark individual traits and states, researchers have also identified several relatively stable communication patterns that impact the quality of one's relationships. These patterns are discussed next.

Darkness and Communicative Dispositions

Communication scholars primarily interested in the individual often focus on traits and situations, such as communication apprehension, rhetorical sensitivity, and communicator style (for further review, see Littlejohn, 1999). Moreover, individual based theories of communication typically examine the cognitions involved in (a) message production (e.g., Delia and colleagues' Constructivist Theory, O'Keefe's Message Design Logics, Green's Action Assembly Theory, and Berger's Planning Theory) and (b) message processing (e.g., Festinger's Cognitive Dissonance Theory, Sherif & Sherif's Social Judgment Theory, and Petty & Cacioppo's Elaboration Likelihood Model) (for detailed summaries of these theories, see Miller, 2005). Each of these theories could be used to reveal dark individual communication processes. Limited space restricts our ability to review each of them and, instead, turns our attention toward two individually based communication patterns that inform dark side scholarship and have garnered much attention from scholars in the field: communication competence and trait verbal aggression.

Communication competence. Admittedly, when the lens becomes so narrowly focused on individual level cognitions and psychological processes, we can lose sight of the communicative nature of such individual functioning. As you will recall, we previously defined dark communication as "the synchronic or diachronic production of harmful, morally suspect, and/or socially unacceptable messages, observed and/or experienced at one or multiple interlocking structures of interaction, that are the products or causes of negative effects (temporary or long term) within the family system." In this section, we focus on the part of this definition related to message production and receipt. In a sense, to claim that a message was constructed darkly or was perceived as a dark interaction infers that the communication was, in some way, ineffective or inappropriate – or both.

The effectiveness and appropriateness of communication interactions has long been a research interest for interpersonal scholars

(Spitzberg & Cupach, 1989). This area of research, known as interpersonal communication competence or interpersonal skills, explores how individuals can choose from a variety of behaviors that comprise characteristics of "good" communicators, among other interests. Although what is perceived as "good" communication may vary across cultures (Philipsen, 2002), most researchers agree that good communicators are aware of how their communication behaviors affect others (self-monitoring), easily adapt their communication to the situation at hand (adaptability), practice empathy, possess the ability to create explanations for another's communicative behavior (cognitive complexity), and communicate ethically (e.g., Spitzberg, 2000). Researchers have discovered that individuals with communication *in*competence (i.e., a failure to exhibit high levels of the characteristics above) and deficient interpersonal skills may "experience a pattern of disturbed relationships that distort normal feedback processes, diminish self-esteem, and create pathways to deviant and risky behavior" (Spitzberg & Cupach, 2002, p. 570). Communication skill deficiency is also correlated with family violence. For example, adults in violent relationships tend to exhibit poor problem-solving skills and neglectful mothers have been found to speak less often and less acceptingly to their infants (for further review, see Anderson, Umberson, & Elliot, 2004).

Trait verbal aggression. In addition to possibly displaying lower levels of communication competence, an individual may also communicate very aggressively. According to Rancer and Avtgis (2006), trait verbal aggression is thought to be a subcomponent of hostility. This relationship to hostility also means that verbal aggression is considered part of neuroticism, a personality trait reviewed earlier. Verbal aggression (VA) occurs when one attacks another person's self-concept as opposed to attacking the individual's argument (Infante & Wigley, 1986). Using VA translates into employing negative communication tactics such as name-calling, accusing, and criticizing one's partner. Some scholars posit that VA occurs when individuals experience threats to their egos; using VA in conflict, for example, can be a means of defending a favorable view of the self (Baumeister, Bushman, & Campbell, 2000). Such an observation was also evidenced in a study by Rill and colleagues (Rill, Baiocchi, Hopper, Denker, & Olson, 2009). Drawing from a college-based dating sample, these researchers found that self-esteem was a predictor of trait verbal aggressiveness. In other words, as a person's self-esteem decreased, their predisposition to use verbal aggression increased. Perhaps most significantly, researchers have found a positive relationship between the presence of VA and relational violence (Infante et al., 1989; Infante, Sabourin, Rudd, & Shannon, 1990) and a negative relationship between the use of VA and marital satisfaction in non-distressed married couples (Payne & Sabourin, 1990). Finally, Leonard and Senchak (1996) also found that husband-dominated relationships (in which the husband does not believe in egalitarian relationships) are characterized by high problem solving, low withdrawal, and high use of marital aggression. These findings reveal that men in these types of relationships quite likely possess all of the characteristics associated with verbal aggressiveness – hostility, neuroticism, and negative emotionality.

In summary, an individual's dark communicative disposition, such as one's level of communication competence and/or verbal aggression, can dramatically affect communication between family members. It is easy to imagine a dark family conflict sparked by one's inability to empathize or one's use of name-calling and the impact of that communication on the receiver. However, we must not forget that interactions are difficult to punctuate – that is, interactants may have differing ideas as to the origin of the conflict at hand (Watzlawick, Bavelas, & Jackson, 1967). Thus, we conclude this chapter by reiterating the importance of time, as it relates to our understanding of the individual's role in dark family communication.

Time and its Effects on the Individual

Thus far, we have reviewed traits, disorders, and communication behaviors of an individual that can negatively impact family communication. Most studies cited identify how a particular trait results in a particular outcome at a point in time. What remains to be discussed, however, is the longitudinal – or diachronic – perspective. That is, how does conceptualizing the individual level and dark family communication change when the element of time is added to the discussion? One way of answering this question is by observing an example from family violence literature. We know that physical acts of violence may follow substance abuse or verbally aggressive conflicts (situations induced by individual level factors). In the face of such a situation, it is natural to take a synchronic perspective; that is we could easily anticipate the short-term consequences of these interactions (e.g., a bruised eye, a hateful exchange of words). However, our approach to dark family communication espouses that we need to conceptualize every dark message – be it verbal or nonverbal – as an *impetus* to dark, as well as an outcome. Restated, viewing a physically violent family episode through a diachronic perspective highlights how dark communication evolves over time. For instance, when living in fear of violence, family members do not have the opportunity to develop adept communication skills (Anderson et al., 2004). Specifically, child witnesses of violence in the immediate family may experience higher levels of anxiety and fear, and lower social competence than children not exposed to familial violence (Anderson et al., 2004). Adult victims of family violence usually have lowered self-confidence and have an impaired ability to maintain healthy relationships. According to Le Poire (2004), adult children of alcoholics often seek relationships with substance abusers because this situation recreates the attachment style they learned as children. It is possible that children of substance abusers may feel emotionally abandoned, which may translate into low self-esteem. Thus, through these research examples, we are able to highlight the longitudinal aspects of dark family communication and the interconnectedness of the individual, family, and time.

Chapter Summary

As we have discussed, individual traits, characteristics, and behaviors impact how people cognitively process incoming messages and construct outgoing ones. With regard to darkness per se, we have learned in this chapter how certain traits and characteristics also are associated with various shades of dark behavior, displaying how (dark) personality can influence (dark) communication outcomes. The material covered in this chapter allows us to understand better why and how individuals may create dark messages that range in their darkness and how these messages can be both positive and negative in their content and impact. By focusing on the darker side of the individual, we have also come to learn how certain traits and states may be associated with the tendency to assign negative (darker) meaning to messages. Such individual tendencies to communicate darkly, in turn, influence the family system. Importantly, while many individual traits are relatively stable, the dark communication behavior associated with them is not. Instead, with effort and time, what may once be considered dark individual behavior and related dark family communication, can be turned into brightness (to apply these principles to a specific family, visit the Moore family in the following case study.

Case Study

Janice watched through the window, sipping her second cup of "coffee," as Bobby hopped up the steps of the school bus. Watching Bobby get on the school bus was just part of her morning routine, consisting of a four-mile run, followed by getting the children ready for school and placing a small peck on her husband's cheek as he rushed out of the door. This morning's routine was a little more chaotic: Lucy dribbled toothpaste on her freshly ironed cheerleading uniform, which now had to be cleaned, and her husband forgot his cell phone, so she had to chase him down the street until he saw her in the rearview mirror. "Thanks, Honey, you're the best," he said, as she slid it into his outstretched hand. He pulled her in slightly, planting a more appropriate good-bye kiss on her lips before pulling away.

She returned home to make sure Bobby made it to the school bus and poured herself a second cup of coffee. It was the first cup of coffee after her morning run that helped prepare her for the ninety minutes of weekday morning chaos; however, it was the second that she enjoyed the most. She took another sip, inhaled deeply, and then turned to her mother.

"Mom, do you need anything before I head downstairs to do some work?" she asked bracing herself for her mother's response.

"No thanks, honey," Trudy responded.

"Just double-checking, mom," Janice replied with a smile as she headed toward the kitchen. She rinsed her coffee cup and placed it in the dishwasher, along with the leftover morning dishes, before grabbing her half glass of orange juice.

She headed to the basement, psyching herself into finishing the illustrations for this year's Mother's Day Greeting Cards collection. She enjoyed this time of day. It also made her feel closer to her father. It brought back memories of times of hiding in her father's workshop and sharing stories of her grandfather. Her dad also taught her his greatest tricks, like how to lock up your "supplies," even in your own studio, to prevent privacy invasion. Her bond with her father grew during the period of time when her mother, Trudy, was pushing her sister, Jolene, to be the ultimate everything. Trudy was also the ultimate team mom for Janice's brother, Thomas.

"Your mother doesn't approve of my drinking, which is why I hide my supplies," he would tell her. "This is our little secret."

She found her magic bottle in her paint bucket, topped off the orange juice glass, and began sketching. She got lost in her head as she drew. She glanced at the clock on the wall. Three hours had passed since she started sketching. Should I go upstairs and fix mom her celery and tuna fish sandwich for lunch? Four hours until Lucy's bake sale. She locked her art

supplies cabinet, exited the room, and locked the door as well. *You've taught me well, Dad. If only you knew how good I have gotten at protecting my privacy. No one has a clue.*
   So she thought.

Discussion Questions

1. What individual traits, characteristics, and behaviors can be identified in this Moore scenario? How might they be impacting relational and familial functioning? What are some specific dark outcomes associated with these individual behaviors?
2. How does an individual behavior, such as alcoholism, impact message construction and deconstruction? Do you think Janice's drinking is impacting her family? If not, why? If so, how?
3. How might time (synchronic and diachronic) influence the family's dynamics as revealed in this scenario?

For Further Thought and Discussion

Theoretical Considerations

1. In your own words, what is the relationship between individual traits, characteristics, and behavioral patterns and dark family communication?
2. How does dark family communication at the individual level impact the family system?
3. Identify a theory that could be used to study dark family communication (e.g., Communication Privacy Management, Relational Dialectics, Systems Theory). How might the information on individual traits and characteristics discussed in this chapter be applied to theory? Does the theory already account for individual differences? Or, could it be expanded upon by adding a more developed individual-based component? If so, how?

Practical Considerations

1. How do you think you would measure on a "Big Five" personality assessment (several scales are available online)? How do you think your own personality impacts communication with your family members?
2. Do you know a family member or a friend with a personality disorder? In what ways do you see the disorder affecting the individual's sending or receiving of messages? How does it affect *your* communication with that individual?
3. Emotions and moods can also affect our communication. How do your personal good and bad days impact how you perceive messages?
4. In what ways do dark individual characteristics affect communication with others in your family?

Methodological Considerations

1. How might you go about studying the impact of one individual's substance abuse on multiple members of the family?
2. What are ways you could design a study on depression and family communication, using either quantitative or qualitative methods?
3. Design a longitudinal study looking at dark individual behaviors and their effect on family communication. What are some hypotheses and/or research questions that you would pose? How would you design the study? Would it be quantitative, qualitative, critical, a mixture? What would constrain you in carrying out this type of study?
4. What ethical considerations need to be taken into account when conducting research on dark individual traits, characteristics, and/or behaviors?

3

The Dark Side of Dyadic Family Life

The one-on-one relationships people have with different members of their families are central to the enactment of family. Common dyadic family relationships include the committed couple, parent–child, and siblings. These dyadic interaction structures, among others, constitute the second interlocking layer represented in our approach to dark family communication. The dyadic structure allows us to examine dark family communication from a variety of vantage points. First, it allows us to highlight how dyads can communicate darkly and, second, how these patterns have dark effects on families over time. Importantly, dyads consist of individuals, so the ways in which individuals impact family communication as discussed in Chapter 2 also influence the dyad. While the angle of the camera is focused in this chapter on the dyad as the unit of analysis, remember that a tighter shot would encapsulate the individual as well (in addition to the remaining two structures – family and society – which receive attention in coming chapters).

Admittedly, there are a myriad of relational couples within the family unit. Our focus in this chapter will be the dark side of family communication enacted by the dyads that have received the most attention by researchers, namely committed couples, parent–child dyads, and siblings. In this chapter, we will review the nature of dark patterns and processes within each of the three dyads.

The Nature of Dark Communication within Committed Couples

No couple is immune from engaging in unhealthy communication from time to time. Yet, as noted by Vangelisti (2002), even though happy couples use more constructive behaviors when compared to unhappy ones, "negative behaviors often are deemed the more sensitive barometer of marital satisfaction" (p. 65). By their nature, these negative communication patterns represent shades of darkness, ranging from the darkest of dark to lighter tints of gray. Concomitantly, these forms of communication can be found within healthy and unhealthy couples, reinforcing the positivity–negativity dialectic inherent to darkness. However, it is important to understand that a rather robust finding within the close relationships literature is the correlation between unhealthy dyadic functioning (e.g., lower levels of relational satisfaction) and the presence of more negative behaviors, including dark communication patterns (for a discussion, see Vangelisti, 2002). In other words, the darker the communication over time, the unhealthier the dyad.

Dark Communication Patterns

Criticisms and complaints. One example of negative behavior and, thereby, dark communication, used by couples is complaints and criticisms. Complaints focus on a specific behavior while criticisms attack the character of the person (Gottman, 1994; Gottman & Carrera, 2000). Complaints are common in relationships and can be healthy; however, over time, complaints may evolve to criticisms and foreshadow relationship demise (Gottman, 1994). Alberts (1988) focused on complaints and found a difference between maladjusted and well-adjusted couples' use of complaints. Specifically, she studied five types of complaints: behavior (e.g., "you are bragging"), personal characteristics (e.g., "you are arrogant"), performance (e.g., "you clean the dishes incorrectly"), personal appearance (e.g., "you are fat"), and meta-complaints (e.g., "you complain too much"). The results revealed that maladjusted couples were more likely to use personal characteristic complaints, negative affect, and countercomplaint responses. In contrast, well-adjusted couples were found to use behavioral complaints, positive affect, and agreement responses. Gottman (1994) also studied couples' use of criticisms over time and found that wives who were on a trajectory toward marital dissolution criticized and complained more than their husbands (who were found to use more stonewalling behavior).

The chilling effect. While complaints and criticisms involve verbalizing discontent, the chilling effect involves the opposite. More specifically, the chilling effect occurs when one partner possesses more punitive or dependence power, thereby increasing the chances that the other partner will withhold grievances (Roloff & Cloven, 1990). Research suggests that, when Partner A is more committed to the relationship than Partner B or when Partner B has more attractive alternatives, Partner A may experience a chilling effect because of his/her dependence upon Partner B and the relationship.

Numerous studies have examined the chilling effect in dating and committed relationships. Examples include one study by Olson and Golish (2002) who found that women experiencing violence eventually emotionally disengaged in order to avoid more violent encounters. As a result, the aggression decreased because of the women's fear of confrontation. Instead of approaching their husbands, participants would instigate a "silent, non-engagement pattern of behavior" (p. 191). Afifi, McManus, Steuber, and Coho (2009) also found the presence of the chilling effect when they examined the relationship between partners' verbal avoidance and satisfaction during potentially conflict-inducing conversations. The researchers discovered that, as compared to the men, women were more likely to report relationship dissatisfaction when they indicated being avoidant due to the perception of their partner's reaction. Another study by Solomon, Knobloch, and Fitzpatrick (2004) examined the chilling effect framework in marital relationships and discovered some important differences in how dependence power was experienced in these marriages (as compared to the past research looking at the chilling effect in dating relationships). Specifically, respondents' commitment was *positively* associated with *expression* of complaints. Additionally, as expected, partners' alternatives were associated with withholding, but only when both partners were equally committed to the relationship, another divergence from the above noted standards of the chilling effect framework. The researchers noted, "Within the more invested and stable realm of marriage, committed spouses may recognize the importance of addressing irritations to facilitate the long-term maintenance of the relationship" (p. 162). These findings underscore the darkness continuum and element of time represented in our definition of dark family communication. Behavior shaded darkly (i.e., expressed irritations) within the moment (synchronic time) can lead to positive, long-term outcomes (diachronic time).

Conflict. All couples fight, leading scholars to assert that conflict is inevitable (Roloff & Soule, 2002). As common as it is, conflict is still considered a problematic relational reality for many – something they would rather avoid. It is also an important communication issue to explore because, as stated by Booth, Crouter, and Clements (2001):

> Couple conflict is an important antecedent of domestic violence, ineffective parenting, and marital dissolution phenomena that threaten the strong functioning of contemporary families and the adults and children living in families.

Most of the darker forms of relational communication discussed above have also been found to occur during conflicts. In addition to those, scholars have identified several other problematic conflict patterns (for a review, see Roloff & Soule, 2002). A group of patterns explained by Gottman (1993, 1994) differentiates couples based upon the ways in which they handle conflict. The typology captures three couples – validating, volatile, and conflict avoiders. Perhaps not surprisingly, Gottman found that volatile couples and conflict avoiders exhibited what could be considered darker forms of conflict management. Both volatiles and avoiders believe that autonomy outranks togetherness; however, whereas volatiles thrive on conflict, avoiders tend to avoid all marital conflicts (Gottman, 1993). Avoiders, as the name suggests, dislike conflict and tend to walk away from it, giving their partner the silent treatment. They also display little negative or positive affect and a great deal of neutral interaction. While not openly hostile (like volatiles), this avoidant pattern has been found to harm relationships (Gottman, 1994). Volatile couples may be considered the darkest of this typology because of their tendency to frequently engage in non-productive fighting. Furthermore, they express a great deal of negative and positive affect and little neutral interaction, underscoring the volatility of these couples. In Gottman's (1993) study, he found that volatile couples, aiming to preserve their individuality, showed negativity in their interactions but also showed affection and humor.

In addition to the couple types, Gottman's (1994) *Four horsemen of the apocalypse* tracks the archaeology of a conflict through four specific behaviors: complaints and criticisms, contempt and disgust, defensiveness, and stonewalling. This pattern works in a sequence that starts with complaints and criticisms (discussed earlier) and ends with stonewalling. While complaining can be healthy (Gottman, 1994), if it continues over long periods, it can evolve into criticism. Thus, the second step of this sequence occurs when one partner perceives complaints to be criticisms, and they feel contempt and disgust with the partner. Disgust occurs when a person has "had enough" which then leads to contempt. Contempt can be identified when a person makes sarcastic comments or insults that reflect judgment of the partner. The next step in the sequence is defensiveness, or, verbal self-defense against personal attacks that are revealed during earlier stages. Finally, stonewalling occurs when the person being attacked tries to defend him or herself and is now withdrawing from conflict. In this stage, partners are no longer trying to work things out.

Empirical support of the stages appears to be consistent and predictive of relationship satisfaction and/or longevity. Moreover, according to Gottman (1994), sex differences exist: men stonewall more than women. This unfortunately leads many heterosexual couples down the path of the demand/withdraw pattern. Other

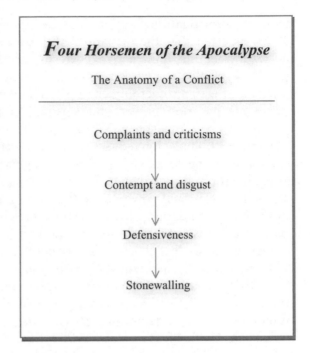

Figure 3.1   Four Horsemen of the Apocalypse

research has identified the linkage between Gottman's conflict couple types and the four horsemen: Busby and Holman (2009), for instance, found that 32 percent of their participant couples ($N = 1{,}983$) perceived a mismatch in their conflict types. Specifically, couples with the mismatched conflict styles of volatile-avoidant experienced more stonewalling than validating matched couples and other mismatched couples.

Demand/withdraw pattern. The demand/withdraw pattern (Gottman, 1994; Heavy, Christensen, & Malamuth, 1995; Holtzworth-Munroe, Smutzler, & Stuart, 1998) is another dark communication pattern, which occurs when one person uses communication that is demanding, while the other person uses tactics to avoid the conflict by withdrawing. Research consistently shows that its presence distinguishes dissatisfied from satisfied couples and can forecast divorce and/or relational violence. Heavy, Layne, and Christensen (1993) asserted that the demand/withdraw pattern is one of the most "intractable, destructive patterns of marital interaction" (p. 16). Typically, the person making demands is female, has less power, and wants something changed. The person withdrawing is often male, has more power, and is usually content with the status quo. Several researchers (e.g., Christensen & Shenk, 1991; Klein & Johnson, 1997) have looked toward a socio-structural explanation when attempting to make sense of these gendered patterns. Such an explanation argues that in heterosexual relationships, women possess less relational power; thus, they are more inclined to be dissatisfied in their relationships and want more change (the demander role). In contrast, men hold more power, are more satisfied, and, as a result, desire less change. Consequently, husband withdrawal "may be a way to maintain the status quo and avoid their wives' demands for change" (Vangelisti, 2002, p. 662). While the socio-structural perspective has received some empirical support, other studies (e.g., Berns, Jacobson, & Gottman, 1999; Caughlin & Vangelisti, 1999; Heavy et al., 1995) indicate that the individuals' desire for change was correlated with which partner assumed the demander role, transcending a purely gendered dynamic. Also, Olson and Lloyd (2005) found in their group of female participants, who admitted to initiating acts of aggression against their male partner, a description of a *withdraw/demand* pattern (reversed linguistical labeling intentional). When describing their justifications for initiating aggression, several women noted that their partners' persistent tendency to withdraw during conflicts prompted the women to issue demands in order to get their partners' attention. Only after repeatedly being ignored and trying more subtle, less aggressive demanding attempts, the women reported resorting to violence.

Demand/Withdraw

One of the most intractable, destructive patterns of marital interaction.

As noted earlier, the demand/withdraw conflict pattern leads to marital dissatisfaction (e.g., Heavy et al., 1995) and the termination of relationships (e.g., Gottman & Levenson, 2000). The pattern is also prevalent in abusive relationships (e.g., Berns et al., 1999). Berns and colleagues found that males demand more often in domestically violent relationships than males in nonviolent but unhappy marriages. Interestingly, however, a few studies have noted some positive effects associated with demand/withdraw or some ways its negative impact could be tempered. For example, Gottman and Krokoff (1989) found that satisfaction increased for wives who used the demand/withdraw pattern. In addition, Caughlin and Huston (2002) found that, while the demand/withdraw pattern and relational negativity were empirically separable, the inverse relationship between the demand/withdraw pattern and satisfaction was buffered by the expression of affection.

Communication Correlates of Relational Power, Control, and Violence. As the above patterns have highlighted, relationships can be characterized by struggles over power, dominance, and control – sometimes expressed, sometimes withheld. Rogers and colleagues' work on relational communication and relational control patterns offer a way of examining these dyadic struggles (e.g., Millar & Rogers, 1976; Millar, Rogers, & Bavelas, 1984; Rogers, 2001; Rogers-Millar & Millar, 1979). The relational approach was grounded in the belief that a "system member" is an influential agent who constructs his/her relationship via "mutually constructed patterns of interrelating with one another" (Rogers, 2004, p. 161). The relational coding scheme was created to examine relational interaction patterns. The scheme accounts for nine different interaction patterns: competitive symmetry (one-up/one-up), complementarity (one-down/one-up), transition (one-across/one-up), complementarity (one-up/one-down), submissive symmetry (one-down/one-down), transition (one-across/one-down), transition (one-across/one-across), transition (one-down/one-across), and neutralized symmetry (one-across/one-across) (Millar & Rogers, 1976). These interaction patterns are used to determine the use of power and control in relationships. More specifically, one-up messages convey dominance or attempts at interpersonal influence, while one-down messages indicate submissiveness. One-across messages are not attempts to exhibit dominance or submissiveness. An example of a study using these interaction patterns found that husbands and wives experienced less relational satisfaction when wives used more one-up messages (i.e., they were domineering; Rogers & Millar, 1988).

Negative messages that tend to attempt direct or assert definitional rights are considered one-up messages (Rogers, 2001). While both satisfied and dissatisfied couples reciprocate one another's positive behaviors, dissatisfied couples tend to respond to their partner's negative behavior with more negative behavior (Vangelisti, 2002). This matching of negative affect is known as negative reciprocity, which has been labeled the "hallmark of marital conflict" because of its association with other dark patterns of communication behavior, marital discord, and even marital violence (Klein & Johnson, 1997).

Although it was not designed for this reason, Fitzpatrick's couple types (1988; Noller & Fitzpatrick, 1992) is another approach to examining how couples negotiate power and control. Specifically, the typology is based upon eight factors that differentiate couples from one another: conflict avoidance, assertiveness, sharing, the ideology of traditionalism, the ideology of uncertainty and change, temporal regularity, undifferentiated space, and autonomy. Fitzpatrick and colleagues identified three different types of couples that vary along these dimensions – independents, separates, and traditionals. In general, traditionals possess a traditional relationship ideology and are quite interdependent. Communicatively, they tend to be non-assertive but not necessarily conflict-avoidant. Independents, on the other hand, hold non-traditional relational ideologies and like their own personal space while also being quite interdependent. They, like traditionals, are not likely to avoid conflict. Separates have been found to hold traditional relational ideologies but non-conventional ideas toward individuality. Therefore, these couples tend to be rather independent and share less with their partners. They also prefer to avoid conflict. With regard to dark behaviors and outcomes, each couple type exhibits some form of unhealthy behavior or experiences some ill effect – especially with regard to the negative effects of power imbalances. For instance, traditional marriages include specialized roles for men and women and are based on male dominance (Steil, 2000). In these families, whether or not the woman works, she is still responsible for the work within the home (e.g., cleaning, childcare) (Steil, 2000), therefore participating in work both in and outside of the home. A study by Kelley (1999) identified that independent wives reported more negative violations of equality-trust than their husbands reported (i.e., the wife's expectation of her spouse versus the actual behavior of her spouse), signaling a communicative struggle to negotiate the non-traditional relational ideologies independent couples often espouse. It appears that separates, who have been found to demonstrate few expressions of affection and report lower levels of relational satisfaction, are the most unhealthy couple within this typology. Separate couples, for example, report less companionship and sharing and characterize their communication as persuasive and assertive (Koerner & Fitzpatrick, 1997). Fitzpatrick (1988) also found that separates were contentious in their communication and used more destructive compliance-gaining strategies as compared to the other couple types. It has been suggested by Fitzpatrick that these couples may be prone to relational violence because of their unhealthy communication patterns.

Unfortunately, another very dark relational pattern involves violence between partners. The violence can include verbal, psychological, physical, economical, and sexual acts enacted by one partner against another. As noted by Anderson and colleagues (2004), "violence is a form of interactive communication. It is motivated by a desire to communicate a message – often a demand for compliance – to the victim" (p. 620). These words and those of others have noted that struggles over power and control are at the heart of intimate partner violence. In an attempt to make sense of these interactive communication dynamics, sociologist Michael Johnson (1995) identified two types of violence against women that were differentiated from each other in part by their patterns of control. These types were labeled patriarchal terrorism and common couple violence. More recently, Johnson (2008) modi-fied the labels and extended the typology to include four types of domestic violence: intimate terrorism, violent resistance, situational couple violence, and mutual violent resistance. The primary way that the couple types are differentiated from one another has to do with the actions of each partner (violent or not) and use (or lack thereof) of control. Mutual violent resistant couples are ones who both use violence and both are controlling. The violent resistant couples include one partner who is violent and controlling while the other partner is violent but not controlling. Intimate terrorism – the one most closely aligned with stereotypical violent relationships – are relationships that include one partner who is violent and con-trolling and the other partner who is neither. Finally, the situational couple violence type includes an individual who may be violent but neither partner is violent and controlling. In one study testing the couple types, Brownridge (2010) found that cohabiting couples were more likely to report situational couple violence and married couples were more likely to report intimate terrorism. Another study by Stith and colleagues (2011) found that vulnerabilities and stressful events led to situational couple violence. Ross and Babcock (2009) found that women did suffer more injuries in relationships that most resembled intimate terrorism, whereas men suffered more injuries when mutual violence existed (relationships similar to the one Johnson labeled mutual violent resistant couples).

Building upon Johnson's (1995) early work, Olson's (2004, 2008) typology of violent couples is an additional way of clas-sifying couples based upon the type and frequency of aggression and three different properties of control. Olson argued that while extant domestic violence literature and typologies, such as Johnson's, appropriately position control at the heart of violent relationships, the scholarship also tends to characterize control as unidimensional, failing to capture its complexity. As a result of such theorizing and empirical testing, Olson (2002) identified three different profiles of couples experiencing aggression: aggres-sives, violents, and abusives (developed further by Olson, 2004, 2008). Aggressive relationships were characterized by lower levels of aggression, dyadic attempts at control, and reciprocated aggression. Communicatively, individuals in these couples expressed a lower tolerance for aggression and meta-communicated about their past use of aggression. This mindfulness and desire to create healthy communication rules set this couple type apart from the others. Violent relationships were defined as those that contained dyadic control, severe power struggles, and high levels of reciprocated aggression and violence. The demand/withdraw pattern (described in more detail in Heavy et al., 1993) was found to exist within these violent relationships as well. Finally, the couples that experienced the most severe violence were labeled abusive relationships; these relationships contained power imbalances, high amounts of verbal abuse (in addition to the physical violence), and domineering–submissive communication patterns.

Both of these typologies demonstrate heuristic value in categorizing violent couples. Yet, as others have argued (e.g., Ross & Babcock, 2009), it is more methodologically sound to conceptualize the patterns constituting each couple types as dimensional rather than categorical. More work needs to be done to identify ways to measure these couples accurately.

At this point, we have reviewed various patterns of dark communication enacted by couples. (See Table 3.1 for a summary.) However, the committed couple is only one dyad within the family. We now turn our attention to dark communication within parent–child relationships.

The Nature of Dark Communication within Parent–Child Relationships

Just like committed couples, parents and children can communicate in unhealthy ways that negatively affect the child and/or the parent–child relationship. Many of these communication patterns are not inherently dysfunctional, but instead contain the potential for darkness and unhealthy relational functioning. We review parent–child communicative interaction patterns that are integral to the enactment of the relationship, focusing on their darker elements. Once again, our review here is not intended to be

Table 3.1. Summary of Dark Couple Communication Patterns.

Dark Communication Patterns of Committed Couples
Criticisms and Complaints
The Chilling Effect
Conflict
Demand/Withdraw

Communication Correlates of Power, Control, and Violence	
Johnson's Violent Couple Types	**Olson's Violent Couple Typology**
Mutual Violent Resistant Couples – both use violence and both are controlling. **Violent Resistant Couples** – one partner who is violent and controlling while the other partner is violent but not controlling. **Intimate Terrorism** – one partner who is violent and controlling and the other partner who is neither. **Situational Couple Violence** – an individual who may be violent but neither partner is violent and controlling.	**Aggressives** – lower levels of aggression, dyadic attempts at control, and reciprocated aggression. (Later broken down into two types: Aggressives and Combatives.) **Violents** – contained dyadic control, severe power struggles, and high levels of reciprocated aggression and violence. **Abusives** – contained power imbalances and severely high amounts of non-reciprocated violence.

exhaustive, but illustrative of the ways in which healthy/unhealthy patterns can co-exist in parent–child relationships (for a more exhaustive review, see Vangelisti, 2004).

Dark Parent–Child Communication Patterns

Communication and parenting. Parents communicatively enact parenting in a variety of ways. To help understand these differences, Baumrind (1971) identified three parenting styles – authoritarian, permissive, and authoritative. These styles vary in degree of darkness, with authoritarian and permissive being the most problematic and authoritative being most positive. Authoritarian parents are commanding, demanding, and directive. Their goal is to control their children's behavior using strict standards and expectations. These parents expect their children to obey them without question, and they do not use reasoning with their children. Permissive parents, in contrast, are quite different from authoritarian parents in that they are undemanding, non-directive, and responsive. These parents act more like a friend to their children, and they give their children considerable amounts of power in the relationship. These parents rarely discipline their children and when they do, they are lenient. Authoritative parents blend the styles of the authoritarian and permissive parents. These parents are demanding yet responsive. They have standards that are expected to be followed and these rules are communicated to their children along with clear reasoning for the discipline. They seek to include the child in decision-making processes that affect the child and avoid harsh punishments by focusing on reasoning and giving support. One study examining parenting styles found that depressed mothers used authoritarian parenting styles more than non-depressed mothers (Pelaez, Field, Pickens, & Hart, 2008). Another study by Dominguez and Carton (1997) related parenting styles with college-aged children's levels of self-actualization. This study found that adult children with authoritarian parents had lower levels of self-actualization than those children with authoritative parents. Baumrind (1996) later noted that these parenting styles contained two dimensions (responsiveness and demandingness) that extended the theoretical understanding of the styles. Specifically, she argued that authoritarian parents are low in responsiveness and high in demandingness, permissive parents display high responsiveness but low demandingness, while authoritative parents are high in both.

Communication and emotion. There are both bright and dark aspects of emotional expression in parent–child relationships. Parents are the main vehicle by which children either learn – or, in cases of emotional dismissive parents, do not learn – how to convey and express emotion (Cupach & Olson, 2006). According to Fitness and Duffield (2004), "family life is a dynamic, intricately patterned kaleidoscope of feelings and emotions, ranging from the most intense hues of anger, hate, and love to the mildest shades of irritation, hurt, and affection" (p. 473). For example, bright aspects of emotional expression include liking and loving (Taraban, Hendrick, & Hendrick, 1998), interpersonal warmth (Andersen & Guerrero, 1998), alleviating emotional distress (Burleson & Goldsmith, 1998), and social support (Barbee, Rowatt, & Cunningham, 1998). However, there is also a dark side of emotion that includes strategic embarrassment (Bradford & Petronio, 1998), guilt and hurt (Vangelisti & Sprague, 1998), and anger (Canary, Spitzberg, & Semic, 1998). Specifically, Grych and Fincham (1990) found that parental anger can negatively impact children who are exposed to overt and intense displays of anger. These children are at risk for problems such as depression, anxiety, and aggression. Gottman, Katz, and Hooven (1997) found similar patterns in their analysis of the relationship between a parent's meta-emotion structure (parent's awareness of his/her own and children's emotions and the parent's emotion coaching) and his/her children's developmental outcomes. Namely, children of parents who practice more "emotion coaching" (coaching children through their emotionality) have been found to have better social relationships, are better able to focus attention, have fewer illnesses, and achieve higher scores in math and reading. Such positive outcomes were not found in children whose parents displayed an "emotion dismissing" style. Instead of helping children learn how to identify and work through their emotion, emotion dismissing parents teach children to minimize and get over their negative affect quickly. Such an approach, according to Gottman and his team, influences children's ability to inhibit negative affect.

Communication and corporal punishment. Corporal punishment (spanking) is one form of discipline that has been examined by many scholars (e.g., Kazdin & Benjet, 2003; Paolucci & Violato, 2004; Pardini, Lochman, & Powell, 2007) and is an especially controversial topic (see Rosemond, 2005, and Straus, 2005 for an example of the debate). The impact of corporal punishment on families, and on children in particular, is mixed, according to research findings. For instance, a meta-analysis of studies on corporal punishment showed that people experiencing this form of discipline are at a small risk for developing behavioral and emotional problems, but are not at risk for developing cognitive problems or acting aggressively toward their peers (Paolucci & Violato, 2004). A more recent review of corporal punishment literature found that spanking and other forms of corporal punishment (e.g., hitting with an object, striking the face) were associated with decreased internalization of morals, reduced quality of parent–child relationships, poorer mental health of the child and adult, more delinquency and antisocial behavior for children, and, for adults, increased criminal and antisocial behavior (Pardini et al., 2007). This study also illustrated how dark family communication works over time: the same study indicated that corporal punishment was linked to the likelihood of being a victim of relational abuse and a higher likelihood of abusing one's partner (Pardini et al., 2007). According to Gershoff's (2002) analysis, children who are spanked tend to be angry, aggressive, and have more stress than children who are not spanked.

On the other hand, the negative associations hold only for specific demographics. Children in many African-American communities, for example, do not experience these same dark outcomes (Deater-Deckard, Dodge, Bates, & Pettit, 1996). Plus, spanking often precedes immediate compliance of the child (Gershoff, 2002). So, whether you are for or against spanking, scholars have argued that the differences in these findings might be illuminated by a closer examination of moderating variables, including age, severity of punishment, relationship between the parent and child, SES, etc. (Paolucci & Violato, 2004).

Dark Parent–Child Behaviors

Almost five children die from child abuse every day in America, and most of these acts – at least 68 percent – are committed by family members.

Child abuse. We are saddened to report that as of 2007, almost five children die from child abuse every day in America, and most of these acts – at least 68 percent – are committed by family members (Childhelp, 2010). Unfortunately, research also contends that at least 30 percent of these abused children will most likely abuse their own children one day, continuing the vicious cycle of abuse (Childhelp, 2010). Statistics such as these present a very dark side of family life. Before discussing the sensitive topic further, however, we must remind our readers that the dyadic level of the definition of dark family communication naturally interlocks and overlaps with each of the other levels, including the individual level. Thus, understanding why a parent would choose to physically, mentally, or emotionally abuse a child requires an understanding of individual cognitive processes and behaviors. As Morgan and Wilson (2007) point out, a

> thorough conceptualization must not only define the nature of damage but also explain how meanings can lead to harm (the mechanism of damage) as well as why parents would talk or act in ways that create harm (the causal mechanism). (pp. 327–328)

Unfortunately, children are subjected to a variety of neglect and maltreatment, including psychological, sexual, and/or physical abuse (for a review, see Barnett, Miller-Perrin, & Perrin, 2005). These acts of violence "can range from a slap on the hand to a cigarette burn on the face to an attack so violent that the result is death" (Barnett et al., 2005, p. 57). Specifically in relation to child abuse, the parent is often seeking some sort of compliance of the child through an aggressive verbal or nonverbal (violent) act. A study of maternal verbal responsiveness, for instance, compared adequate, neglectful, and abusive mothers of infants (Christopoulos, Bonvillian, & Crittenden, 1988). While adequate mothers used subtle means of gaining compliance (e.g., requests) with their children and used longer and more grammatical statements, abusive mothers used more sentence fragments and more rejecting statements than adequate and neglectful mothers. Palazzolo, Roberto, and Babin (2010) found that children of verbally aggressive parents had higher levels of victimization and perpetration. Furthermore, children of verbally aggressive parents were more fearful, anxious, or dismissive of their parents than children of nonverbally aggressive parents (Palazzolo et al., 2010).

Undoubtedly, child abuse is one of the darkest patterns of family life. It includes acts that leave us shocked and uncertain of what to say next. Interestingly, research indicates that the abuse of a child by a parent is not the only direction of abuse in the parent–child dyad. We turn to a brief discussion of parent abuse next.

Child-to-parent abuse. With the rapid increase of 65 years and older persons in our population, it is not surprising that we are seeing increases in elder abuse, which is most often perpetrated by partners and adult children (Barnett et al., 2005). Unfortunately, limited information is known about elder abuse, and experts disagree on causes, victimization rates, and perpetrator profiles. Part of the problem, according to Barnett and colleagues (2005), is "attitudes toward the elder and disabled tend to discourage victims from reporting abuse, thus keeping the problem hidden. Many elders themselves hold counterproductive attitudes, such as 'What goes on at home stays at home.'" (p. 372). Even though we may not have conclusive evidence on the etiology of elder abuse, we do know that it exists and is in need of further exploration by dark side family communication scholars.

Another "dirty little family secret" is adolescent-to-parent abuse. In her study, Eckstein (2004) discusses the pain felt by parents who experience verbal, physical, and emotional abuse at the hands of their adolescent children. These parents felt that the emotional abuse was the most severe form of adolescent-to-parent abuse. Threats stated by adolescents during emotionally abusive episodes were perceived as real by parents if children had previously abused the parent. The previous physical abuse made the threat more realistic and caused severe emotional distress in parents. In some cases, parents would tell themselves that the child's verbal abuse was acceptable because the child loved them enough not to abuse them physically or emotionally. Many of the parents felt shame and embarrassment and remained silent about such abuse.

We now move into our final discussion on family dyads: the sibling relationship.

The Nature of Dark Communication within Sibling Relationships

Like the previous relationships we have discussed so far, sibling relationships can take on a variety of forms. They can include biological siblings, half-siblings, stepsiblings, adoptive siblings, foster siblings, or fictive siblings (Button & Gealt, 2010). Sibling relationships can be created through blood ties, adoption, or stepfamily creation. Regardless of type or formation, sibling relationships can be special, loving bonds or agitating, troublesome attachments, or something in between. As noted by Sillars, Canary, and Tafoya (2004), "sibling relationships are a significant source of conflict for most children and adolescents . . . and they have heightened significance because children cannot put an end to their sibling relationships" (p. 415). We address two of the darker sibling interaction patterns next.

Dark Sibling Communication Patterns

Verbal aggression. Research points out that siblings' use of language toward each other can be destructive, disconfirming, or antisocial (Myers & Bryant, 2008). The use of verbal aggression can be in the form of teasing, which not only affects the level of trust between siblings (Tevan, Martin, & Neupauer, 1998), but is also associated with less relational satisfaction (Anderson et al., 2004).

In addition to teasing, dark communication from another sibling can include name-calling, insults, withdrawal, physical acts or threats, repudiating the relationship, negative affect, and unfair comparison (Myers & Bryant, 2008). Despite the type of message received from one sibling to another, the transmission of the message results in hurt feelings. Harmful messages hurt more from family than non-family members, especially when the source of the message believes in what they are saying (Young & Bippus, 2001). This may explain why sibling verbal aggression even in its more minor form can be so hurtful.

Sibling abuse. Sibling *rivalry* may be common in some families but to be considered abuse, the emotional and physical impact as well as the long-term consequences must be taken into account (Button & Gealt, 2010). Kettrey and Emery (2006) found that 70.5 percent of participants either experienced or perpetrated severe violence toward a sibling. Eriksen and Jensen (2006) identified individual, dyadic, and familial patterns that increased or decreased the likelihood of sibling violence. First, with regard to factors that decreased sibling violence, research shows that as children grow older, the violence decreases. Moreover, higher family income and dual-career working partners are both associated with less sibling violence.

Conversely, if parents are discussing separation or divorce, sibling violence increases. Eriksen and Jensen (2006) note that parent-to-child violence is associated with increased sibling violence while marital violence is not. This means that the observation of violence has less of an effect than the experience of violence from a parent to their child. In addition, the more mothers physically punish their children, the more likely the children are to act violently toward their siblings, and the more husbands lose their tempers, the more children act violently toward each other (Eriksen & Jensen, 2006). Another cause of sibling violence is maternal attention to either child. If a mother pays more attention to one child over another, the siblings are more likely to participate in violent interactions (Stafford & Dainton, 1994). Children pay close attention to acts of favoritism and are sensitive to differences in treatment among siblings.

Chapter Summary

Dyadic life within the family certainly contains shades of darkness that can become lighter or darker over time.

In this chapter we examined darkness with romantic family partners, parent–child relationships, and sibling relationships. Each of these relationships exhibit shades of darkness. For instance, romantic familial partners may have to deal with violence, criticisms, and complaints, or the chilling effect, to name a few. Parent–child relationships may include dark issues of physical and emotional abuse (from parent to child or child to parent), negative forms of parenting, and harmful spanking. Sibling relationships may have to deal with abuse and verbal aggression.

We must remember that no summary is complete, however, without drawing the other levels of our approach to dark family communication – individual, familial, and societal – into the discussion. For example, individual members' drug or alcohol use could impact their approach to interpersonal conflict, criticism, or complaints. Society's normalization of sibling rivalry impacts the interpretation of siblings' aggressive tendencies. Are acts of aggression "normal" rough play between a brother and sister or unacceptable violent behavior? Up to now, social norms have interpreted such behavior as normal sibling interaction. Recently, however, a wind of change has blown in, questioning the normalization of such violent behavior. We can also see the impact of familial patterns when looking at the intergenerational transmission of aggression, or, more specifically, when we read evidence of abused children growing up to abuse others. Yet, time can work in favor of individuals and family pairs too. Couples can learn how to better handle their conflict, and parents can learn to use more constructive forms of discipline. As we have demonstrated, dyadic life within the family certainly contains shades of darkness that can become lighter or darker over time. Throughout this discussion, you may have considered how the interactions of a family dyad impact the family as a whole. We examine this very concept in the upcoming chapter. Before turning to that chapter, however, apply this chapter's concepts to our Moore family.

Case Study

Janice pulled up at the entrance to the band building to drop off Freddie's marching band uniform.

"Thanks mom," he said. "This means a lot to me. I don't know where my head was this morning."

"Where it always is after a tense night of arguing with your father about school applications?" she suggested. Freddie leaned in to her car and gave her a quick squeeze. Then he opened the back door and got his band uniform.

"By the way, mom," he began. "Steve is staying with us this weekend. His dad is pulling the graveyard shift again."

"You know Steve is always welcome," she replied. "But thanks for the heads up. Remember to stop by and say hello after the halftime show. You need to clear the air with your dad."

"Okay," he grumbled. Freddie headed back to the band building, listening to the sound of his mom's Element turn around on the gravel parking lot and head toward the football field.

I understand why he wants me to go to West Point or Annapolis. He wants me to have options, give back to the country, and not have to worry about money. He wants me to have discipline and honor. But what he doesn't know is that I won't be marrying a female cadet or a girl from one of the local colleges. I really thought dad would have realized by now that I am gay.

"Hey Steve," he shouted as he entered the changing area. "Mom says she's looking forward to you staying with us this weekend. She also said that we should go over and say hi after the halftime show. Maybe we can get some free munchies off of them."

"Sounds good," Steve replied. "See you outside."

Freddie watched as Steve pulled on his marching hat and joined the rest of the brass section for warm-ups. Freddie quickly began to change out of his jeans and tight black t-shirt. *You think he would notice that I dress like Simon Cowell, considering how much he watches American Idol with Lucy. Now I have to play nice all weekend.* Last night's argument, episode 742 in the Fred vs. Freddie verbal sparring, began as a result of his acceptance into SCTA.

"I've been accepted into the Savannah Conservatory for the Arts, the best art school in the country, dad," he had said as the dinner conversation hit a hum, after Lucy's blow-by-blow recall of the pyramid collapse at cheerleading practice.

"That's a nice pipe dream," Fred replied. "Have you contacted the Senator's office about a letter for the West Point application?"

"I don't want to go to West Point. I don't want to join the military. I want to do something with art. I'm good at art." He noticed his mother's small smile as she took another sip of wine and pushed her food around the plate.

"You're good at art, but there is no future in art. Art will not pay the bills. Art will not put food on the table. Art will not cover the rent. I will not foot the bill if you go to art school. Are0you a sissy – a mama's boy? Or are you a man?"

"I am a man that wants to go to art school," Freddie snapped. Fred jumped out of his seat quickly, spilling Bobby's glass of milk, and lunged toward Freddie. Before Lucy could swallow her piece of meatloaf, Fred slapped Freddie across the face, the blow sending Freddie to the floor. He sat there as his father towered over him.

"I am giving you options. Options that I never had," Fred began, his voice getting louder as he progressed. "You will go to West Point or Annapolis. You will join the military. You will become an officer. You will . . ."

"Fred, that's enough. May we finish dinner?" Janice interrupted, glad that it was her mother's bingo night and that Steve was not there.

"You hush up and stay out of it. I am the head of this family. Finish your wine," he sneered. Janice quickly diverted her eyes away from her husband and oldest son. "And you," he began turning back toward Freddie. "If you plan to live in this household until you are eighteen, then you will do what I say." He grabbed Freddie by the arms and lifted him. "And if not, then get the hell out of my house you worthless piece of crap." Fred gave his son one final shove into the dining room wall and went back to his meatloaf. Bobby sat in stunned silence, while Lucy choked back tears.

Freddie left the dining room, most of his dinner untouched. Lucy snuck him a sandwich later.

"What are you going to do about school?" she asked as she placed the sandwich on his desk.

"Probably just go through the motions. I'm stuck here until my birthday or graduation, so I really don't have a choice."

"Then what are you going to do? Can't you just tell dad that you're gay?"

"Lucy, coming out of the closet to dad is not even an option. Even now with the military accepting gays. He thinks I'm worthless now. How is me telling dad I'm gay going to change that?" he asked.

"You don't have to bark at me, big brother. I just hate how all this is going. I just want everyone to be happy." She said as she slammed his door shut. Lucy's last comment hung with him even today.

"You coming?" Steve shouted breaking Freddie from his memory. Freddie grabbed his mellophone, rushed to meet Steve, and then headed outside to join the rest of the band for warm-ups. Football season was officially underway.

Except I play in the band, not on the field, Freddie thought. *Just one more reason for my father to be disappointed in me.*

Discussion Questions

1. Janice and Fred displayed several unhealthy forms of communication in this story. What dark couple communication pattern(s) discussed in this chapter can you identify? How would you describe their conflict management? Do you see signs of any relational violence? If so, what are they?

2. Building on what you learned in chapter 2, how do you see individual-level issues affecting Fred's and Freddie's relationship and their parent–child communication? Also, how might

Janice's alcoholism (an individual-level issue) be impacting the dyadic interactions in the family?

3. How would you describe the sibling communication in this story? Healthy? Unhealthy? Explain your answer.

For Further Thought and Discussion

Theoretical Considerations

1. What are some examples of how individual characteristics (discussed in Chapter 2) would influence dyadic interactions with the family? How might time (synchronic and diachronic) impact these interactions?
2. What dark dyadic processes do you feel are in need of further scholarly attention?
3. We examined three main family dyads in this chapter and expounded on their characteristic dark communication patterns and processes. What other family dyads can you think of that might experience dark communication and how?
4. Recently, research has been conducted on adolescent-to-parent abuse. How do you see the element of time impacting that dyadic interaction?

Practical Considerations

1. How has sibling rivalry affected you or your friends? How would you differentiate sibling rivalry from sibling abuse?
2. What advice would you give to a couple locked into the demand/withdraw pattern? How might they get out of such a dangerous relational dynamic?

Methodological Considerations

1. How could the Four Horsemen of the Apocalypse be captured in a study of couple conflict?
2. Identify another darker form of sibling communication. How

would you design a study examining this pattern? How would you use quantitative and qualitative methods to examine that phenomenon?

3. What methodological obstacles would you need to consider prior to studying children who were physically or sexually abused by a parent?

4

Familial Interaction Structure and the Dark Side

Families are like puzzles. Each part contributes to the overall picture. Occasionally a piece is lost or damaged, changing the puzzle's composition forever. This mirrors family processes. For instance, when two members of the family fight, it affects the entire family. Or, when a family loses one of its members to death or through divorce, the entire family – not just those members directly involved – is undoubtedly affected.

That family picture is the focus of this chapter. As you will recall from the previous chapters, we discussed dark side communication from the individual and dyadic perspectives. Now, in this chapter, we will learn that the dark at individual and dyadic levels can also darken communication within the entire family system. To continue the camera metaphor discussed in Chapters 2 and 3, we widen the lens's angle to capture the family as a system with *family* as the unit of analysis.

Over time, individual and dyadic levels of family communication contribute to a family's overall communication patterns, thereby establishing family norms for future communication and behavior (Vangelisti, 2004). For example, what if families' norms include excessive verbal or physical aggression? How is the family – as a whole – affected? Our intent here is to further explain these processes and how they could be considered dark or associated with dark outcomes within the family system. In so doing, our discussion will include a review of three family level theories and several communication processes of family communication. We will conclude the chapter with a discussion of how time factors into the dark communication at the level of the family system.

Family Theories Shaded Darkly

Theories help explain how things work – whether it be explaining how children form attachments with their primary caregiver and the lifelong impact of those attachments (individual-level theory) or how romantic couples communicatively enact different forms of relationships (dyadic level theory). Often, family theories help explain, for example, how individuals learn to communicate and behave within the family, or how dyads within the family come to form patterned ways of interacting. This section, however, is devoted to discussing more macro theories/models that address family interaction at the *family* level. There are numerous family level theories that have dark elements within them, including, for instance, a family-based model of intimacy (Foley & Duck, 2006), a typology of family functioning (Sturge-Apple, Davies, & Cummings, 2010), family interaction relationship types (Chao, 2011), and the Resiliency Model of Family Stress (McCubbin & McCubbin, 1993). We encourage interested individuals to explore each of these frameworks in more depth. In this chapter we will explore an additional set of theories – Family Systems theory, Family Communications Pattern theory, and the Circumplex Model.

Family Systems Theory

Up to this point, we have discussed dark communication within families from the individual and dyadic perspectives, focusing on how just one or two people within the family may create or maintain dark family communication. However, it is important to realize that, from a systems perspective, individuals' dark communication within the family must be observed wholly to gain greater understanding of why dark communication continues to exist (Minuchin, 1984). That is, the parts affect the whole (von Bertalanffy, 1972). Our conceptualization of dark family communication stresses the importance of viewing dark family communication as a phenomenon not limited to just one or two family members. Instead, entire family systems may be shaded darkly. Galvin, Dickson, and Marrow (2006) define a system as "a set of components that interrelate with one another to form a whole" (p. 311). We begin our theoretical discussion by expanding upon this metaphor and discussing family systems theory (Minuchin, 1984; von Bertalanffy, 1950, 1968, 1972).

Scholars assert that families are systems (Vangelisti, 2004) and that "these systems evolve through developmental stages, are composed of many parts, and are situated in particular contexts" (Vangelisti, 2004, p. xv). As such, families are interdependent, whole, develop patterns, vary in degree of complexity, are open, contain complex relationships, and are considered goal-oriented entities (Galvin et al., 2006). These seven characteristics are central to the systems metaphor. However, because of space issues, we focus our review on three characteristics: interdependence, patterns, and openness.

Families . . .
are interdependent, whole, develop patterns, vary in degree of complexity, are open, contain complex relationships, and are considered goal-oriented entities

---

First, families are interdependent, meaning that a change in behavior of one family member will affect the rest of the family and have a lasting impact (Galvin et al., 2006). Interdependence also affects the family throughout the members' lifetimes. When newborns are brought home, for example, they are dependent on their parents or guardians for caregiving. Throughout adolescence and young adulthood, the degree of interdependence may change, as teens are still reliant on their parents, but parents may find their lifestyles and schedules altered by their teenagers. Finally, as the child grows into adulthood and starts his/her own family, the older adult parents may become increasingly dependent on the now-adult child. As these examples suggest, family interdependence has implications for our family communication habits and behaviors. Naturally, interdependence between family members becomes even more complex when one considers interdependent relationships between diverse family type members, such as blended families, or between members as families expand (e.g., in-law relationships; Serewicz, 2006).

Next, families create patterns. One type of family pattern is the communicative enactment of rules and rituals (Baxter & Braithwaite, 2006a; Galvin et al., 2006). As summarized by Baxter and Braithwaite (2006a), rituals have been linked to positive health and well-being for individual family members. Unfortunately, however, some family patterns, rules, and rituals can contain shades of darkness. Galvin et al. (2006) suggest that occurrences of incest, battery, or even domestic violence may be a continuation of family patterns or behaviors that were witnessed as a child and then repeated as an adult.

Finally, how open a family is to various contextual and structural forces influences the communicative life of the family system. In other words, what is going on outside the family will impact the internal workings of a family. One study illustrates the effect of boundary openness on family functioning. Kohler, Grotevant, and McRoy (2002) conducted a poignant study that examined the connection between how adopted adolescents seeking information about their birth family influenced the context of their adoptive family. The researchers found that the more preoccupied the adolescents became with finding information about their birth family, the less they trusted their adoptive parents. Because of their intense emotions, these adolescents reported that they became more detached from their adoptive family and perceived less security. A fascination with an issue outside of the family (birth family) impacted the internal context of the family (less trust). As the context changes, families within this context change how they communicate (Ballard-Reisch & Weigel, 2006), demonstrating how open family boundaries may alter the family system and color it a shade of gray.

Family Communication Patterns Theory

Another family level theory is Family Communication Patterns. Koerner and Fitzpatrick (2006), building on the extant work of McLeod and Chaffee (1972), explained that families have an inherent need to achieve psychological balance and understanding of each other. In order to achieve shared meaning, then, the scholars argued that families tend to develop fairly stable and predictable ways of communicating. Koerner and Fitzpatrick posited that families achieve this in two ways: by conforming to the views and values of other members (conformity), and by openly discussing an issue and coming to a shared conclusion (conversation).

The two dimensions of family conformity (high/low) and conversation (high/low) can be combined into a 2×2 structure, resulting in the identification of four family types. These family types can be measured using the Revised Family Communication Patterns scale (Koerner & Fitzpatrick, 2004; Ritchie & Fitzpatrick, 1990). The first family type, those high in conformity and high in conversation, is the consensual family. In a consensual family, there is pressure to agree and to preserve the existing hierarchy within the family and also an interest in open, exploratory communication. The second family is the pluralistic family, which is high in conversation and low in conformity. This family is characterized by open, unconstrained discussion that involves all family members and a wide range of topics. The third family is protective, which is low in conversation and high in conformity. This family is characterized by an emphasis on obedience to parental authority and by little concern for open communication within the family (Koerner & Fitzpatrick, 2004). Characterized by few and often lifeless interactions between family members on a limited amount of topics is the laissez-faire family: low in conversation and low in conformity. In a laissez-faire family, members are emotionally divorced from the family, participate in little communication with others, and only discuss limited topics (Koerner & Fitzpatrick, 2004).

Much empirical work has illustrated the heuristic value of FCP, the corresponding typology, and its relationship to dark family communication. Schrodt, Witt, and Messersmith (2008) point out that family communication patterns "have small but meaningful association with a host of individual family member outcomes" (p. 262), including those that are shaded darkly. For instance, a family's use of conformity and communication behavior influences individual behaviors such as exposure to violence on television, deception, use of power, and conflict behaviors, to name a few (Schrodt et al., 2008).

In addition, scholars have identified relationships between family communication patterns and conflict (Koerner & Fitzpatrick, 1997), children's attitudes to sex and alcohol (Booth-Butterfield & Sidelinger, 1998; Koesten, 2004) and eating disorders (Botta & Dumlao, 2002). An interesting finding that these studies have in common is that low levels of conversation and high levels of conformity lead to negative outcomes, such as in Botta and Dumlao's study. These researchers found that a dysfunctional family environment led to the daughters' negative self-image, which, in turn, contributed to poor interpersonal communication skills and a greater chance the daughter would develop an eating disorder. More specifically, they found that daughters whose families did not encourage them to speak freely and openly communicate their feelings developed an eating disorder. In general, Botta and Dumlao's results revealed that bulimia developed as a reaction to growing up in a hostile and controlling environment, anorexia was a result of a family environment that allowed very little freedom, and binge eating helped daughters deal with a variety of emotional states. Finally, Miller and Day (2002) examined the link between parental communication patterns and college student's thoughts about suicide. In families where a father maintained high levels of family conformity and a mother expected perfection, daughters were more likely to contemplate suicide.

The Circumplex Model

The final theory that we will review in this chapter is one that also assists in shedding light on how dark communication affects the family system. Olson and colleagues (2000) developed the Circumplex Model, which highlights patterns of cohesion, flexibility, and communication within the family. First, cohesion is the level of togetherness a family feels; the emotional bonding each family member has toward other family members. There are four levels of cohesion ranging from high to low, respectively: enmeshed, cohesive, connected, and disengaged (Olson, 2000). Representing the two ends of the continuum, disengaged and enmeshed levels of cohesion are considered to be unbalanced because families are emotionally distant (disengaged) or require strong levels of loyalty (enmeshed). In enmeshed families, individuals are strongly encouraged to remain within the family unit and there is little communication with the outside world (Olson, 2000).

Next, flexibility examines the amount of change a family can handle (Olson, 2000). Change may include a change in leadership, role relationships, and relationship rules. Flexibility has four levels, once again ranging from high to low: chaotic, flexible, structured, and rigid (Olson, 2000). According to Olson and DeFrain (1997), the families at the extremes of the continuum – chaotic and rigid – can function adequately in the short term but experience more difficulty adapting over time either due to their chaotic flexibility or their rigidity. In contrast, the flexible and structured types are considered much more balanced and better able to adapt to change over the family life course.

The four levels of both flexibility and cohesion combine to form a 4×4 typology, resulting in sixteen types of couples and family relationships. In general, the families fall into one of three categories: balanced, mid-range, and unbalanced (Olson, 2000). Balanced families contain the two central levels of cohesion and flexibility. They have been found to be happier and better functioning across the family life cycle when compared to unbalanced families (two extremes on cohesion and flexibility). Importantly, the differences between balanced and unbalanced families do not rest solely on the dimensions of flexibility and cohesion but also on how communication factors into the situation. Communication, the third component of the model, then fulfills a facilitating dimension between cohesion and flexibility. Communication is measured by focusing on the family's "listening skills, speaking skills, self-disclosure, clarity, continuity tracking, respect, and regard" (Olson, 2000, pp. 149–150). Not surprisingly, balanced families have more positive communication skills compared to unbalanced families (Olson & DeFrain, 1997).

Related to the goals of this chapter, the Circumplex Model provides communication scholars interested in dark side communication an opportunity to examine how dark family communication operates in unbalanced families. In general, unbalanced families lack communication skills, are less healthy, and cannot function adequately during the life course of the family system because they lack the necessary skills needed to help the family achieve a more balanced state. The point of the Circumplex Model is to find a balance of cohesion and flexibility; however, dysfunction can occur when there is too much cohesion or too much flexibility (e.g., Carnes, 1989; Clarke & Hornick, 1984).

In summary, the Family Systems theory, Family Communication Patterns theory and the Circumplex Model offer a strong basis for examining how family communication becomes normalized over time and how these patterns relate to other behavioral outcomes. Also, by identifying families by their types, scholars are able to examine how an imbalance in one component (e.g., high conformity, low cohesion) contributes to dark communication and dark outcomes.

Family Level Communication Processes Darkly Shaded

In this next section, we explore several communication based processes that contain brightness and darkness. Due to the focus of the book, we will be more inclined to discuss the dysfunctionality of these processes.

The Communicative Elements of Family Privacy

Petronio's Communication Privacy Management theory (CPM; Petronio, 2002) is a theoretical framework that examines how individuals manage their privacy by constructing privacy boundaries. One can also see shades of systems theory, family communication patterns, and the circumplex model discussed earlier within this framework. Importantly, although the management of privacy is not inherently dark, it certainly can contain darker elements. Let us begin with a review of the theory and then discuss more about how it can be useful in studying dark family communication. Privacy rules are developed to help control the flow of information from one person to another (Petronio, 2002; Petronio & Durham, 2008). The formation of boundaries may occur on interior (i.e., occurring within the family unit) and exterior levels (i.e., occurring between family members and outsiders; Caughlin & Petronio, 2004; Petronio, 2002). Therefore, privacy boundaries are established within families and also between a family and outsiders. In the former instance, privacy boundaries are established between individuals within a family, delineating different configurations of individuals who know and those who don't and rules for maintaining information flow. In the latter case, the entire family must work together to control the information from spreading to individuals outside of the family (Caughlin & Petronio, 2004). Since the focus of the current chapter is the family as a whole system, we will examine these family level privacy rule orientations.

As noted by Petronio (2002), boundary management can become stabilized in families. Petronio describes three resultant congruent patterns within families (family level and individual level are the same) and the degree to which their boundaries are (im)permeable (see Petronio for additional discussion of families with incongruent privacy orientations). First, there are families that are highly permeable, loosely controlling their privacy boundaries. According to Petronio, these families are very communicatively open with outsiders and with each other. She also asserts that such openness is likely associated with being highly enmeshed or interdependent, thereby sacrificing autonomy. In contrast, some families construct impermeable boundaries, making it very difficult for outsiders to share with this family private information. It is hypothesized that families such as these are more likely to keep secrets, withhold information, and restrict access in general. Correspondingly, Petronio argues that individuals in this type of family may be more likely to be disengaged from each other. They also may be less able to adapt to change because they keep their boundaries so tightly closed, reducing their ability to learn from others how to be adaptive and flexible. Third, there are the moderately impermeable families, showing flexibility in their willingness to share private family matters with outsiders. Individuals within these families are more likely to follow a family-derived set of rules for privacy rule orientation, figuring out what can and cannot be shared with others.

One way researchers have studied family privacy management is by examining *family secrets*. Bok (1983) defined family secrets as events or information that family members hide from each other or from those outside the family. The prevalence of keeping a family secret is surprising: in one study by Vangelisti and Caughlin (1997), 98 percent of approximately 700 respondents recalled a family secret (i.e., the intentional concealment of information).

The communication processes and decisions involved with family secrets are laced with darkness. Family secrets kept by the whole family from outsiders ("whole-family" secrets), or kept by a few family members from other members ("intrafamily" secrets; Karpel, 1980) may leave some individuals feeling guilty, burdened, and distressed from the psychological weight they carry (Afifi & Caughlin, 2005, 2006; Afifi, Olson & Armstrong, 2005). Studies show that when secrets are kept within the family system, individuals hold negative feelings about their families (Vangelisti, 1994; Vangelisti & Caughlin, 1997).

On the other hand, secret revelation also has its drawbacks (Afifi & Steuber, 2009). Family members may struggle with the desire to reveal information while grappling with how to most effectively reveal the secret while protecting the self and the recipient (Afifi & Olson, 2005; Afifi et al., 2005). In general, research suggests that the circumstances in which secrets are disclosed are less flexible than for other forms of information (Vangelisti & Caughlin, 1997). Moreover, some families, more than others, are less able to handle the consequences associated with the concealment and later revelation of a secret (Poulos, 2009).

Family Rituals

Anyone who can recall hearing something like "We always go to Applebee's on Friday nights," "Everyone in the family attends church on Christmas eve," "Cake is a must when it's your birthday!" is probably no stranger to family rituals. We assume a stance toward rituals similar to Baxter and Braithwaite (2006a) who assert that ritual is a *"genre of communication events"* (emphasis in original, p. 260). More formally, these same authors define family ritual as a *"voluntary, recurring, patterned communication event whose jointly enacted performance by family members pays homage to what they regard as sacred, thereby producing and reproducing a family's identity and its web of social relations"* (pp. 262–263, emphasis in original). Thus family rituals are a way of preserving family history, creating an idiosyncratic identity, and building bonds.

At first glance, rituals as a *dark* family process might appear out of place. Our standpoint is that many rituals are not often inherently dark, but some certainly can be and some can be perceived to be. Take for instance a child who is beaten every time her father comes home drunk – a dark recurring, patterned communication event which produces a family identity but one that is filled with violence and betrayal rather than joy and hope. Or, the man suffering from depression, who cannot bring himself to attend the jolly family Christmas party, is another example of the dark side of family rituals. We assert that more research needs to be done in examining these dark family rituals in order to broaden our understanding of this important family event. It is important to acknowledge that there can be a dark underbelly of family rituals that most would prefer not to acknowledge, let alone study. Yet, all too many people experience them, thus compelling us as dark side family researchers to better understand how family rituals can contain shades of darkness as well as the brightness that has been heretofore studied.

Stress, Strain, and Family Darkness

All families experience some form of stress (Turner & West, 1998). For instance, scholars have examined family communication surrounding the illness or death of a family member (Knafl & Gilliss, 2002), the stress involved in caring for a family member stricken by a devastating illness (Arrington, 2005), and familial conflict when a spouse falls ill or has a mental disorder (Arrington, 2005; Solomon, Cavanaugh, & Gelles, 2005). Similar stress-related communication ensues due to the passing or sickness of a child (Hastings, 2000; Toller, 2007, 2008). Death in the family is a stressor for which families cannot always plan; it results in a period of change and uncertainty – and necessarily impacts family communication (Turner & West, 1998). Nilsen (2010) explained that losing her father and her only sibling to a drunk-driving accident impacted how she communicated (positively or negatively) with her mother, as well as extended family members.

Importantly, dark shades of family communication in these instances may not be intentionally dark: for instance, the sheer nature of the situation may influence family members to communicate more aggressively or sharply than usual. How that stress is handled, however, appears to differentiate families from one another. Boss's (2002) Contextual Model of Family Stress is one theoretical approach to analyzing how families as a whole deal with the stress they encounter. The model looks at the interaction of three factors (the stressor event, the resources available, and the assigned meaning or perception of the situation) on a potentially stressful situation. More specifically, the model proposes that when a family experiences a stressor, they evaluate what resources they have to handle that particular stressor. After evaluating their resources, the family members assign some sort of meaning to the stressor, perhaps questioning "what does this mean?" or "how will this impact our family?" How the family answers these questions will impact the degree to which they experience stress or discomfort, emphasizing the role perception and attitude have on stress management. In other words, if the individuals involved focus on the stressor more negatively, then they will be more inclined to feel more stress than family members who view a similar situation more positively. Families change over time – new members may be added, other members lost, and life-changing events occur. It does not matter if the change is specific to one or two members of the family; the very nature of families as systems requires the impact of the change to be felt by each member in some capacity. Each stage of the family life course brings a new set of stressors (Turner & West, 1998). Boss (1988) points out that not all families respond the same way to the stressors but that these stressors are inevitable over the course of the family life structure.

Chapter Summary

As this chapter comes to a close, we urge readers to recall that dark family communication, according to our definition, (a) entails not a black or white decision, but instead, a spectrum of darkness, (b) is often perceived as dark by those *observing* and not those *participating* in the communication, and (c) cannot be wholly understood if separated from the familial, historical, and social context in which it occurred. Applying chapter content to our approach to dark family communication, we see that various family-level theories and processes are either dark in and of themselves or, more commonly, possess dark elements. Our focus here has been on the *family* as a unit of analysis, but we need to remain mindful that *individual* and *dyadic* interactions constitute the family unit. This means that the individual and dyadic interlocking structures are influencing and being influenced by dark family processes – all of which can change over time. Revisit the Moore family to see these dynamics in action.

Case Study

Janice pulled her car in the driveway behind Fred's as she began to rattle off directions to her two youngest in the back seat. "Bobby, make sure you get in the bath right away to get that mud off of you. Lucy, no phone or computer until your homework is done. I know it is Friday night but your grades are slipping, and we don't need another reason to upset your father."

The reunion of the family after the halftime show did not go as Janice would have liked. She went into "mother bear" mode as she watched the second half of the game, vowing to protect the other two from her husband's wrath. Now with Steve here this weekend, she had to do everything in her power to keep things calm.

"Mom, do you need any help?" Janice asked Trudy.

"No, thank you. I think I'll just go to my room and finish my book. Sweetie, you are doing well with those kids. I know he doesn't see it and that you don't always see it, but you are," Trudy replied. "Your husband is just going through a rough time. Freddie will survive." She hugged her daughter and headed into the house.

Janice looked at her watch. She locked her car and headed into the house – and then hesitated. She waited until the garage door closed halfway before she opened the door to the winter storage closet, dug out the bottle of tequila, and took a shot. Then, she popped the last piece of gum into her mouth and went into the house, stopping right inside the door. Fred was sitting at the kitchen table.

"Freddie is not going to Savannah," he began. "We are not going to talk about this. There is no room for conversation." Janice stood there, her mouth partially open as if she was going to reply but stopped when Fred yelled, "If you want me to keep your secret from your children, then you will be with me on this, Janice. Did you enjoy the tequila shot?"

He exited the kitchen before she could answer. She heard

him lock the door of his den as she slumped into the seat he just abandoned at the kitchen table.

Bobby broke her from her stunned silence: "Mom? Are you and dad getting a divorce? I heard him yelling at you and I'm scared that he is going to divorce you. Billy's parents got a divorce. He says his mom cries all the time and now his daddy has a new girlfriend. Is dad gonna get a girlfriend?"

"Bobby, no and no. No, we are not going to get a divorce. We're just having a bad night. And no, dad is not going to get a new girlfriend. Now come over here, kiss me good night, and you head up to bed. No more yelling tonight, I promise."

Bobby did as he was told. He was no sooner gone when Lucy entered. "Are Freddie and Steve coming home tonight or are they going to hide out until dad finishes his latest tantrum?" she asked. "I need help with my algebra homework and Steve is a wiz at math."

"You know what sweetie, why don't we do that algebra tomorrow? How about you and I share that pint of Ben & Jerry's that is in the freezer and watch a movie? Mom and daughter bonding time."

"Mo-om . . . that is so lame, but sure. Anything to get out of homework. Can I text on my phone while we watch the movie?"

"Put the phone on vibrate."

Janice and Lucy snuggled onto the couch, the pint of Ben & Jerry's between them – with two spoons.

"Mom, can I ask you a question?"

"Sure, honey."

"Why do you drink so much?"

Janice's eyes widened. "Why do you think I drink so much?" she managed.

"I smelled your coffee while you chased after dad this morning. Do you drink so dad will love you? Or is it so you can handle dad when he goes on his physical and verbal tantrums toward Freddie? Will life be better once Freddie is gone? Do you think dad is mad at Freddie because you drink and he can't get you to stop? What will happen to Bobby and me if you keep drinking and then have an accident?"

"Woah, honey, that's a lot of questions. I –" She paused. "I just don't know, honey," she began. She sat there looking at Lucy's perfect skin, her long blond hair. "I honestly don't know." She hugged her daughter tightly, smoothed her hair down her back, and thought *Oh god, what if my drinking is the cause of Fred and Freddie's fights?*

Discussion Questions

1. Using the Circumplex Model and Family Communication Patterns, how would you describe the communication of the Moore family?
2. How are the individual and dyadic interaction structures influencing the family dynamics? What impact do these individual and dyadic elements have on the overall family system?
3. Do you see elements of the bright-dark dialectic in this family scenario? That is, what aspects of the family communication in this scenario are shaded darkly? Which are brighter?

Further Thought and Discussion

Theoretical Considerations

1. Choose a particular dark communicative behavior (e.g., intimate partner violence) and discuss how the actions of the individuals and the couple impact the family system.
2. We have discussed various theories and processes that can address how dark communication can be addressed within the family system. What additional theory or process might be useful in studying dark communication within the family?

Practical Considerations

1. Consider how you think your family would be classified according to Family Communication Patterns theory and the Circumplex model. What do you think communication scholars would conclude about your family's communication behaviors?
2. Many counselors and therapists use evaluative measures based on elements of the Circumplex model to assess family communication in order to diagnose family functioning. If you were a family therapist using these assessments, how would your knowledge of the dark family communication influence your interpretation of the assessment results?

Methodological Considerations

1. Assume you are a family communication scholar interested in studying family conflict. What methodological obstacles do you think you would encounter? How could you handle those obstacles?
2. After reading the information from this chapter, how would you study family level darkness?

5

Dark Family Communication in a Context of Darkness

Thus far, we have explored the first three levels of our approach to dark family communication: the individual level, the dyadic level, and the family level. In this next chapter, we examine the *social interaction structure* – the final piece of our discussion of dark family communication. When we interact with our families, it is easy to forget the impact society has on our interactions. In fact, the impact of society is something that we family communication scholars often forget too! The truth is, families do not exist in a vacuum: there is always a context to consider. These external influences – structures like the media, religion, cultural norms, historical time periods, etc. – mold our thoughts and perceptions as we grow up. Eventually, our attitudes, beliefs, and values (sometimes referred to as our *worldview*) become such a part of us that we overlook or take for granted where they came from in the first place. Critical communication scholars would call this our *ideology* – or the idea that we accept a worldview unconsciously, without ever really reflecting on where these core beliefs originated or why we hold them so dear (Anderson, 1996).

Narrowing this idea further then, those same structures that influence our views of life in general, also influence how we think specifically about family (Braithwaite & Baxter, 2006; Coontz, 2000; Popenoe, 1993; Stacey, 1990). Whether it is our determined boundaries for family inclusion, the "proper" way to interact with a family member, or how we judge the communication of our own or others' family members, chances are high that those opinions and evaluations reflect our ideology.

In this chapter, we will look at some of the main tributaries of societal influence: culture, media, and religion and politics. The influence of one's historical location on family attitudes and communication is also examined followed by a discussion of media's effect on violent behavior. Finally, because of the close ties between religion and politics, we bundle these two elements together to illustrate their impact on dark family communication.

Before diving into the chapter, we wish to offer some reflexivity – that is, an opportunity to turn the tables on ourselves – first. Just as you come in to reading this book with your own attitudes, beliefs, and values about family, so do we as authors. For instance, our beliefs about who makes up a family might be broader than others' beliefs. Or, our belief that all families contain some darkness may be a statement with which you disagree. As a result of such differences in philosophical orientations, some of the examples we offer here as society's "dark" family communication messages may not be perceived as such by you, or your neighbor, or your professor, for instance. But the fact that these different opinions may cause you to disagree with us only highlights the importance of this chapter all the more.

Cultural Influences on Family Darkness

The overarching social context influences which family interactions are considered socially or morally acceptable and harmful. It also serves as a model – and not always a positive one – for how to behave and communicate in relationships, including relationships with our family members. The term "culture" has been widely defined (Diggs & Socha, 2004). For the purposes of this chapter, we use the term culture to represent "learned patterns of behavior and attitudes shared by a group of people" (Martin & Nakayama, 2010, p. 84). Thus, for this discussion, cultural differences refer to both inter- *and* intra-cultural differences in one's family upbringing. Our working definition of culture (Martin & Nakayama, 2010) calls to mind three particular aspects of culture: geographic location, socio-cultural influences, and historical period. We delve into each of these in the following section to demonstrate instances of culture influencing dark family communication – both between and within families.

Culture

learned patterns of behavior and attitudes shared by a group of people

---

Culture and family communication. Our specific cultural context (geographic location) bears tremendous weight in defining communication norms within and across families. For example, research has shown that geographic region influences communication with family elders (Giles et al., 2003), one's emotional distance with family members (Georgas et al., 2001), one's parent–child communication (Mackey, 1988), and even how one operationalizes the term "family" (Singh, 2009). The roles that particular individuals assume in the family may also differ based on country of residence. For example, in some countries, child caretaking responsibilities more commonly fall to the paternal grandparents than the maternal grandparents when parents are absent (Chen, Short, & Entwisle, 2000).

Further support for specific cultural based differences in family interactions can be found within the communication conflict literature. For instance, some scholars (e.g., Cai & Fink, 2002) are particularly interested in assessing how families in individualistic cultures – or, those cultures more "self-focused" – differ from the conflict styles of those in collectivistic cultures – cultures that place an emphasis on the group or the society. Also exploring cross-cultural families, Shearman and Dumlao (2008) discovered that American families tended to communicate more often and openly than Japanese families. They also found that Japanese families placed more value on silence, self-control, and concern for the other's feelings, more so than American families. Thus, we can begin to see how the same conflict might look very different in an American family and a Japanese family when these cultural differences are brought to light.

Individuals' geographic region, however, also influences their evaluations of *others'* ideas and behaviors regarding family. For example, the practice of genital surgery, or Female Genital Cutting (FGC) varies across cultures and influences attitudes about and communication within families. Akintunde (2010) explains that FGC usually occurs on young girls between the ages of seven days old and fourteen years old, and is commonly practiced in African and some Middle Eastern and Asian communities. Although FGC functions as a way to promote group identity, its ties to the family values of the culture are clear: most women must undergo this procedure to "preserve family honor" and "further marriage goals, including sexual enhancement for men" (American Academy of Pediatrics, 2010, p. 1089). Those females remaining uncut are often considered unmarriageable and sexually loose (Rudman & Glick, 2008). Naturally, the beliefs and attitudes about family underlying this procedure – and the procedure itself – reflect a much darker norm when compared to North American families' attitudes and beliefs. However, some North American communicated beliefs and practices, such as male circumcision, might be found equally dark by families in other cultures.

Influence of historical period. The historical perspective also influences how we approach familial relationships and assign meaning to the interactions within families. Sometimes we have to "zoom out" to truly get a sense of time's dramatic impact on family communication issues. In most cases, the family communication issues we find "bright" today, might not have been perceived that way by our grandparents in decades previous. For instance, during the early to mid twentieth century in the United States, individuals may have been less likely to interpret racially based hate messages within the family as dark. However, in today's world, one would hope that more families (albeit not all, unfortunately) would judge this type of rhetoric as hateful – and thereby harmful, morally suspect, and socially unacceptable – in other words, dark. Another example of how time has changed the perceptions of interracial marriage comes from a 2007 Gallup poll. The poll indicated that only 17 percent of Americans disapprove of interracial marriages (between Whites and Blacks) (Carroll, 2007). But consider how one's answer to the question might change based on the element of time: In 1991, the rate of disapproval was as high as 42 percent, and this rate pales in comparison to the 94 percent of individuals who disapproved in 1958 (Carroll, 2007). In fact, interracial marriage was prohibited by law in most states until 1967 when the Supreme Court deemed anti-miscegenation laws (those laws banning interracial marriages) unconstitutional. The relevance of this scenario to dark communication has been demonstrated in the literature, particularly in studies showing that supportive family communication regarding an interracial relationship correlates with lower levels of perceived differences in family relationships and more relationship satisfaction for the couple in question (e.g., Soliz, Thurson, & Rittenour, 2009); stated in another way, when our family supports our choice in marital partner, all parties fare better. When we do not have that support, negative outcomes follow.

In addition to historical perspective, the media greatly contribute to our ideas of family and family communication. In the following section, we review the influence of media on dark family communication. We acknowledge that the line between culture and media is a blurry one, as the influence of one on the other is often reciprocal; however, for the purposes of this chapter, we separate the two to examine more closely their unique influence on family communication.

Media Influences on Dark Family Communication

The exposure to media, and in particular, television, influences communication about families, as well as within the family (Wilson & Morgan, 2004). In the interest of space, we limit our discussion to television programming here, due to its pervasive influence on all ages (Gerbner, Gross, Morgan, Signorielli, & Shanahan, 2002). In particular, a combination of exposure to families on television and personal experiences influences how youth develop schema about what to expect in families and how to respond to events within the family (Wilson & Morgan, 2004). A lively debate exists about the degree to which viewing violence on television leads to violent behavior. Some find that it does; others find it does not; others find both, noting the need to study context and a variety of other variables. In this section, we review studies showing the negative impact of violent media consumption, but want to caution readers that we are presenting only one side of the coin.

With regard to research showing the harmful effects of violent media consumption, Murray (2008) found from a review of multiple studies that those who watched more violence on television used more aggressive tactics when solving interpersonal conflicts (for a review, see Murray, 2008). Another study documented 707 television viewers over a period of seventeen years, from childhood to adolescence, and found a significant relationship between television viewing and violence later in life (Johnson, Cohen, Smailes, Kasen, & Brook, 2002). The effect was strongest in boys, however. This study found the relationship between television viewing and violence in later life existed even after controlling for other factors, including previous aggressive behavior, psychiatric disorders, parental education, and childhood neglect. Similarly, Krcmar and Vieira (2005) found that exposure to aggressive acts of violence on television had a negative effect on children's moral reasoning, even after controlling for the age of the child. The authors explained how watching aggressive television programs may lead children to use similar strategies in their own relationships in the future:

> Schemas for aggression are derived from those representations that we have seen; therefore, exposure to unpunished violence, executed by attractive models or unattractive villains, with no real consequences may help children create schemas wherein aggression is an appropriate and effective means of solving problems. (p. 270)

We need to reiterate what we posited earlier; the findings discussed above are controversial and debated by media scholars of all types. Gunter, Harrison, and Wykes (2003) assert that

> Researchers in the United States, in particular, have claimed that the debate is closed given their belief that they have proven that a causal

link exists between violence on television and viewer reaction. Their claim that television violence leads to desensitization, imitation, and fear has been broadly accepted in the United States and underpins both public policy and public debate about the problems of violence on television. However, the question about effects of television violence has been further complicated by new emphasis on the importance of context. This new focus gives rise to a whole new raft of uncertainties about the way audiences respond to violence on the screen and should be taken into account when discussing issues of censorship, warnings, advisories, and content ratings. (p. 255)

Television is not only responsible for sending dark messages *to* the family, but also for sending dark messages *about* the family (Potter, 2005). Society is constantly bombarding us with messages about family ideals. For instance, "one-big-happy-family" shows like *The Brady Bunch* (Schwartz & Rudolph, 1969) or Disney movie cartoons like *Cinderella* (Geronimi, Jackson, & Luske, 1950), with a prominent "wicked stepmother" as chief villain, contribute to our ideas about family interaction, especially in blended families (Barnett et al., 2005; Coleman, Ganong, & Fine, 2004). Negative perceptions of stepparents in modern-day families relate to how they are portrayed in movies (Claxton-Oldfield & Butler, 1998). More recently, television shows have provided new perspectives on family, such as *Modern Family* (Levitan, Lloyd, & Winer, 2009), where the patriarch, who is a white male, is portrayed as having a difficult time adjusting to his son's gay lifestyle, marries a Colombian woman half his age, and has a stepson who has intelligence beyond his years. One hopes that more diverse social messages about different kinds of families impact individuals and push the boundaries of what constitutes healthy family functioning.

The Influence of Religion and Politics on Dark Family Communication

Religion and politics play an important role in how we communicate in our families as well. Religion and politics are often difficult to separate, despite our government's attempts to keep them apart. For example, family issues, such as abortion, are often tied to religion, but also the focus of much political debate. Families serve as the vehicle by which many of us first experience religious and political beliefs and values (see Christiano, 2000). Importantly, religious and political influence may be a two-way street; that is, parents and caregivers may be influenced by their children just as children are often influenced by parents/caregivers (McDevitt & Chaffee, 2002). Religious and political structures that guide so much of our daily behavior also give us a good idea of how individual family members should communicate and behave with each other (Cornwall, 1988; Galvin, 2004). Additionally, examining a family's religious and political context allows us to examine the forces that may infiltrate and determine current and future family interactions, including interactions linked to patriarchal gender relations (Barnett et al., 2005; Galvin, 2004) and children's attitudes and behaviors regarding gender roles (Davis & Pearce, 2007). For example, some families from strong Protestant backgrounds view certain traditional gender roles in the family – such as the man providing for his family while the wife stays home with the children – as service to God (Baker, Sanchez, Nock, & Wright, 2009).

Surprisingly, the influence of religion and politics on family is an understudied area in the communication literature; the door is wide open for those wishing to investigate how religion and politics impact families (Davidson & Widman, 2002; Diggs & Socha, 2004). Although research is limited, it is easy to imagine how religious and political ideologies influence family interactions. In families who do not conform to each other's religious or political views, for instance, family conversations can be rocky at best (e.g., McDevitt & Ostrowski, 2009). Typically, however, families hold similar religious and political beliefs and this is often true across the lifespan. Pearce and Thornton (2007), using the 31-year Intergenerational Panel Study of Parents and Children ($N = 909$), discovered that mothers' religious characteristics (e.g., church attendance) at the time of a child's birth related positively to that child's family ideologies in both childhood and young adulthood.

Naturally then, similarities in important values may catalyze "bright" communication among family members. However, this is not to say that families who *agree* on one particular religion or political party are free of any communication related darkness.

If family members uniformly adhere to a particular political or religious view, one might logically expect less conflict regarding those issues in that family, and thus, less opportunity for dark communication to occur. The new question becomes: can "bright" communication ever become "dark"? When you take the meaning-making process portion of our definition of dark family communication into account, the answer is yes. Ultimately, the meaning-making process helps us remember that what is dark on one's spectrum of family communication may be a few shades lighter in another's opinion. Let us look at an example to illustrate this further.

Currently, the Christian Identity movement is a hate group in America. Although lacking a national governance, supporters of Christian Identity – mostly small churches comprising extreme, fundamentalist Christian families – believe that the Anglo-Saxon, Celtic, Scandinavian, Germanic, and associated cultures are the racial descendants of the tribes of Israel. Thus, by extension, all white Americans are believed to be descendants of God, and all Jews, the descendants of Satan; followers of the movement use the Bible, and the book of Genesis in particular, to justify this belief (Barkun, 1997). Many in the Christian Identity movement believe that before God's kingdom can be established on earth in the Second Coming, a war (or, "cleansing process") will ensue between the white and nonwhite races. The implications of these beliefs has earned the Christian Identity a spot on the Federal Bureau of Investigation's "most dangerous hate group" list for several years (Tuft & Holleman, 2000) – in 1999, on the verge of Y2K, they held the number one ranking. An FBI report entitled *Project Megiddo* (Federal Investigative Bureau, 1999) concluded that adherents to the Christian Identity movement were considered one of the nation's greatest foes due to their "potential for violence" and "pairing up with . . . members of the Ku Klux Klan and other right-wing groups" (p. 16). Nearly a decade later, the movement continues to grow stronger under the guidance of Pastor Thom Robb.

Of particular importance to this chapter is the weight the Christian Identity places on parents teaching the "truth" to their children (see Baiocchi-Wagner, 2010a). The movement proudly operates a website dedicated to "White Pride" homeschooling, offering resources for worried parents who do not wish their children to be socialized into a racially integrated society ("White Pride Homeschool Resource Center," n.d.). In a 2008 Christian Identity publication called *The Torch* (Robb, 2008), Jason Robb warned Denver, Colorado parents of the upcoming National Conference for LGBT Equality with this statement:

> Hold onto your children tight – homosexuals will be out in full force. These homosexuals will be eyeing your children. There will no doubt be individuals that attend these conferences are are [sic] members of the Man/Boy club that actively promotes men having sexual relations with boys. (p. 15)

Radio broadcasts, conferences, and other websites affiliated with the movement offer similar resources to parents looking to teach their children about the "dangers" of mixed-race politics, friendships, and marriage. The second author of our book was particularly stunned by a for-purchase decal (see Figure 5.1) that was produced by Kingdom Identity Ministries, warning women about dating outside of their race (Baiocchi-Wagner, 2010a).

For us, and perhaps for many reading this chapter, these statements are shocking and disturbing. From our viewpoint, we would label parents communicating hatred toward other races and sexualities to their children as "dark," certainly. However, parents in the Christian Identity movement view communicating these values of white superiority to their children as a parental duty – an indication of sound, loving parenting. Just as your parents may have thought it important to instill certain values and morals in you (e.g., respecting your elders, standing up for what is right), Christian Identity parents believe they have the same responsibility. From their perspective, anything communicated that goes

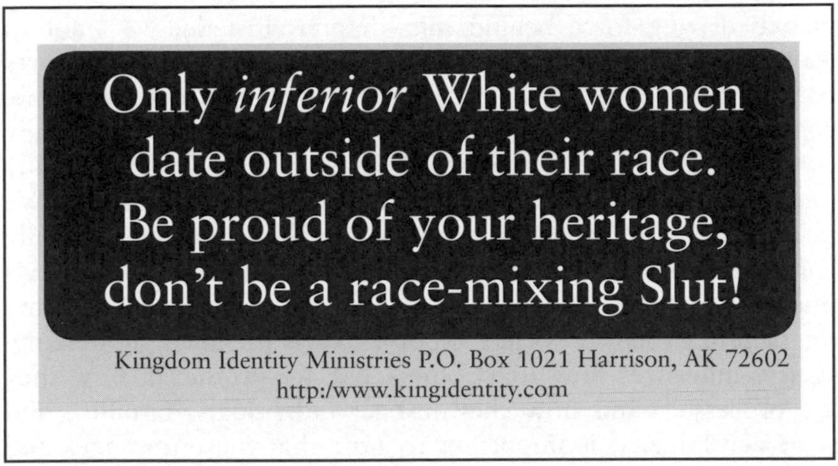

> ## Only *inferior* White women date outside of their race. Be proud of your heritage, don't be a race-mixing Slut!
>
> Kingdom Identity Ministries P.O. Box 1021 Harrison, AK 72602
> http:/www.kingidentity.com

Figure 5.1 Negative Message About Interracial Dating

against that value set – the support of a child's interracial marriage, for instance – would be defined as dark.

Of course, the Christian Identity movement and other hate groups across the globe are extreme examples. The underpinning dark ideal of racial intolerance, as previously discussed, is one example topic that we currently experience in our society.

In summary, we have reviewed several elements related to the fourth level of the dark side of communication: societal structures. By now, you have probably noticed how the elements discussed here – culture, media, religion and politics – are not mutually exclusive in their influence on families. For instance, US political figures often cite religious scripture in their campaign speeches. Religion and politics are both presented to us in the forms of various newscasts and primetime television episodes. And this is not just true of American culture, but of several cultures as well, such as in the Middle East, where television, family, religion and government form interdependent relationships (Azadarmaki, 2008). Culture in some countries is strongly dependent on the dominant religion. Importantly, knowing *which* element is responsible for a dark family communication episode is not the pivotal driving force behind this chapter. Instead, we want to leave you with an understanding of how these societal structures contribute to one's ideology, which contributes to dark family communication and perspectives. If we do not analyze dark family communication within its particular context, we will never fully understand how dark communication operates in the family. We believe that our theoretical approach to the dark side of family communication provides a mechanism for understanding society's impact on the sense-making processes involved. As an interlocking interaction structure, society becomes a site for meaning making: society influences how (dark) messages are produced, how they are processed, and how they impact individuals, families, and society-at-large. It is important to note that these messages and their effects can contain shades of darkness, as well as change over time. Read how these dynamics may be experienced by the Moore family.

Case Study

"What's the deal with your dad? Why does he want you to join the military so badly?" Steve inquired of Freddie as they shared a pizza after tonight's performance.

"What do you mean?" Freddie hesitated, knowing that how he responded might unleash some family secrets. Steve had been staying with the family off and on for years, since his mother died from breast cancer. Steve's father never remarried, throwing himself into his work after the death of his wife.

"You know what I mean. Seriously, man, you could have cut your family tension with a knife tonight. And your old man hardly said two words."

"He's mad at me because I don't want to join the military."

"That sucks, man, but seriously, why does he care so much?"

Freddie drew in a deep breath and knew things couldn't get any worse. He thought of Steve as his brother, given the amount of time Steve spent at the house. "Ok, dude. My

---

dad's parents started off with nothing. My grandparents met at some function having something to do with Vietnam. My grandmother came from a proud military family, and her father was very supportive of the Vietnam movement. My grandfather, well technically he could be considered a draft dodger. He became a hippie, traveling around the country, so he didn't have to go fight in Vietnam. They met at some event, and the legend is it was love at first sight. My grandmother became pregnant, and her father forced a non-church wedding. Not only did they have different political views, my grandfather was a Presbyterian, while my grandmother was a strict Catholic. The Catholic church would not perform the ceremony. My dad came from nothing, and he keeps pushing me to be better than previous generations."

"Oh."

"Yeah, for you and me, it isn't a big deal. Our generation is cool with relationships of different colors, different races, different religions, and same-sex couples." Once again, Freddie paused to see if there was a reaction from Steve. "However, this was a no-no for my great-grandfather. My grandparents made things work. My granddad had connections all around the country and landed a job with a start-up computer company. He and my grandmother found a two-bedroom apartment and made things work. My dad worked his way through college. Despite having nothing, his parents supported him and pushed him to go farther than they did. He was a first-generation college graduate. My dad wants me to go further than him. In a way, he was born with a bit of my great-granddad's stubbornness. It is his way or the highway."

"Well that explains some of tonight's tension," Steve sighed, knowing that he asked the question but just wasn't expecting the family drama. *How could I have spent every other weekend and two weeknights with this family and not know any of this?* "We should head back to your house before the situation gets any worse. Hell, wouldn't want your dad to think we ran off and eloped, would we?" Steve said as he playfully punched Freddie in the arm.

The boys paid their bill, exited the pizza place, and headed home. The only sound on the way came from the radio. As they pulled up to the house, Freddie noticed that the only light that was still on came from his father's den. He braced himself for what to expect when he entered the house.

In the den, Fred turned to Trudy, who entered while he was deep in thought enjoying a glass of scotch. "Drinking seems to be the go-to medicine in this house," Trudy said.

Fred looked up with a sly grin. "I guess you're right."

"Penny for your thoughts."

"It may cost you more than a penny, Trudy. Freddie is making me so frustrated right now."

"You know, he's just a boy just trying to grow up to be the man he wants to be, like you did."

"But I started with nothing. My parents had nothing. I want him to have so much more."

"Don't you see he already does?"

Fred stopped, stared at the ice at the bottom of his glass as Trudy walked away. "I love him so much. I love her so much, but I just feel like they're keeping something from me, like I don't know the full story of what's going on with them."

Silence filled the room, the only sound was two teenage boys shuffling down the hallway toward their room.

Discussion Questions

1. What dark social processes are present in this situation with the Moores?
2. Drawing upon past chapters, what dyadic communication patterns or individual characteristics do you see in this family interaction?
3. As an expert in dark family communication, what advice would you give to the Moores for how to better handle what is happening in their family right now?

For Further Thought and Discussion

Theoretical Considerations

1. Talk through the characteristics and assertions from Chapter 1 as related to the contents of this chapter. How does society impact dark message construction? Processing? What kind of dark effects can result from dark societal messages? What role do the individual, dyad, and family play in this message construction and processing?
2. What shades of darkness seem most relevant to an exploration of society's role in dark family communication? What examples exist that demonstrate a positivity–negativity dialectic?
3. The Christian Identity Movement was one example given that demonstrates how dark family communication is often a construction based on another's perception. What other family memberships are often constructed as "dark" that could lead to "dark" family communication (as perceived by others)?
4. Society continues to be influenced by introductions of new media, technology, and factors. Moreover, families are affected by some of these changes, such as recessions. How might our conceptualization of dark family communication work to reflect these changes?

Practical Considerations

1. What are some socially influencing factors that affect your family? Do they have dark and/or bright effects?

Methodological Considerations

1. Using the characteristics and assertions of dark family communication discussed in Chapter 1, design a study that reflects how society might impact family communication. What method would be best used to capture society's influence on family?
2. The Christian Identity is a great example of darkness among

a religious group. What is an example of darkness in politics that affect the family? How could a researcher examine this phenomenon? What methods could they use?

3. What ethical implications arise for studying a researcher-perceived dark family structure?

6

Concluding Thoughts

> Family life is messy, and, as much as it is filled with happiness, love, support, and nurturance, it also contains sadness, hurt, conflict, isolation, and struggles.

As you have learned from reading this book, family life can be filled with shades of darkness. Within some families, the shade can become a permanent dark tint, coloring negatively all individuals and interactions within the family unit. For other families, however, the shade of darkness is temporary, only capturing a fleeting moment of life. It is even possible that for some, darkness can propel them into lightness – into a more constructive, healthy family life. The possibilities are endless because darkness is omnipresent. That may sound overly cynical to some of you. However, we subscribe to the same belief as others (Roloff & Miller, 2006; Vangelisti, Maguire, Alexander, & Clark, 2007) who state that family life is messy, and, as much as it is filled with happiness, love, support, and nurturance, it also contains sadness, hurt, conflict, isolation, and struggles.

In order for our theorizing to reflect accurately family interactions, family communication scholars must capture both sides of this positivity–negativity dialectic. Toward that end, you will recall that in the opening chapter we posited a definition of dark family communication and five characteristics with corresponding

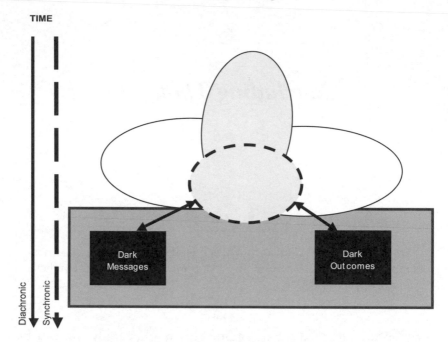

TIME

Diachronic

Synchronic

Dark
Messages

Dark
Outcomes

Figure 6.1   The "What" of the Darkness Model

assertions that have framed our entire discussion of this family phenomenon. As a reminder, dark family communication was defined as the *synchronic or diachronic production of harmful, morally suspect, and/or socially unacceptable messages, observed and/or experienced at one or multiple interlocking structures of interaction, that are the products or causes of negative effects (temporary or long term) within the family system"* (Baiocchi et al., 2009, p. 11). We also described four characteristics that expounded on the definition with their corresponding assertions.

At this point, we would like to explain how the definition, characteristics, and assertions all work together to form what we call the Darkness Model of Family Communication. Let us begin with the first characteristic, the dark communication itself (the "What" of our model; see Figure 6.1). We see dark communication as containing verbal and nonverbal messages that have harmful, morally suspect, and/or socially unacceptable outcomes. These messages also

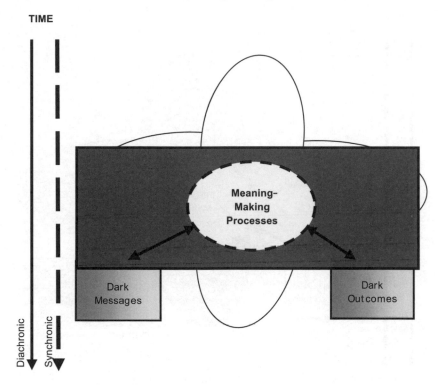

Figure 6.2   The "How" of the Darkness Model

contain shades of darkness and can be dialectical in their positivity and negativity.

Next, our model seeks to reflect visually the meaning-making processes (Characteristic 2) that are involved with all communication, and, more salient to the current discussion, dark communication (see Figure 6.2). Of particular importance to dark communicative processes is the idea that the communication described in the paragraph above is actually or perceived as being intentionally or unintentionally sent and received. Furthermore, the meaning-making processes involved with these messages are made by the individual communicators or observed by uninvolved individuals, extending the meaning-making process to a broader, more socially regulated realm.

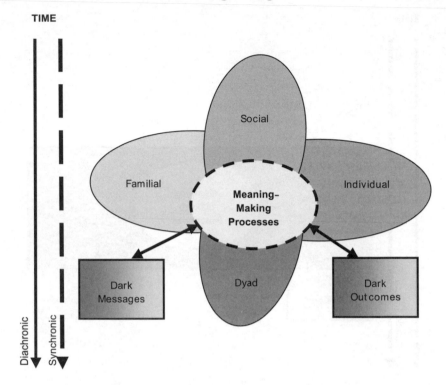

Figure 6.3   The Darkness Model of Family Communication

Drawing upon an ecological approach, the four interlocking structures (Characteristic 3) of the definition and corresponding model are key sites where meaning is being processed. In other words, the communication and the meaning making associated with it are occurring at the individual, the dyadic, the familial, and the social levels. All of these structures influence communication and meaning making and are influenced by them as well. Then, finally, all of these processes must be contextualized by time – synchronic and diachronic (Characteristic 4).

In sum, the model (see Figure 6.3) reflects what constitutes dark messages, how they are assigned meaning, where the meaning making is situated structurally, and what impact they have (on those within and outside the family system) across time. The four interlocking interaction structures become both sites for communication interactions (e.g., units of analysis) as well as sites for meaning making. In other words, individuals are the interactants who structure the communication, and the meaning assigned is a by-product of the structuring influences involved.

We feel that the Darkness Model of Family Communication and the contents of this book serve as heuristic tools to further theorize on the topic. Specifically, it is our hope that the definition, characteristics, and assertions along with the visual model can become theoretical grounding for understanding related scholarship and seeing ways in which it can be extended. The chapters in the book explored dark family communication at the Darkness Model's four interlocking structures – the individual level, the dyadic level, the familial level, and the societal level. Within each chapter, we reviewed how family communication processes impact and are impacted by each of these levels. We also discussed how the element of time, another component of the Darkness Model, was related to the communication issues inherent to each structure. Although many publications have focused on the broader domain of dark interpersonal relationships, to the best of our knowledge, articulating the dark side of *family* communication remained understudied. Our goal was to provide a text to scholars and students alike, solely devoted to family communication and the dark side. This contribution, however, continues to highlight the growing need for continued investigations into families' dark communication. Guided by the Darkness Model, our purpose in this concluding chapter is to provide a starting point for future investigations into the dark side of family communication, to introduce potential methods for studying dark family communication, and to offer a few concluding remarks about the Model itself.

The Future of Dark Family Communication Research

Although you surely have a few ideas of your own by now, we offer a few topic suggestions here. These topics have begun to gain in popularity already, but many scholars agree that more exploration in these areas is needed (e.g., Coontz, 2003; Galvin, 2004; Jennings

& Wartella, 2004). We concede that family communication studies would certainly benefit from these inclusions, but dark family communication studies in particular are needed also.

Understudied family stressors and their communication correlates. Families are experiencing many stressors today that impact their functioning – many of which were never experienced by earlier generations. For example, parents are having to worry about online predators forming relationships with their children; children must negotiate a much tougher world of bullying with the increased use of social media as a weapon of aggression; and the boomerang generation's return home is affecting family functioning. Communication struggles are also apparent in families dealing with the stress of caring for their children with disabilities, such as autism or ADHD, or for a parent diagnosed with cancer. How families communicate before, during, and after the stressful situation is important for all family communication scholars and certainly of import to those of us interested in the darker, more troublesome aspects of family life.

In addition to the stressors noted above, we believe that dark side scholarship needs to attend to family challenges across the lifespan. For example, research indicates that an increase in general life expectancy necessitates interaction among multiple generations of family members (Silverstein & Marenco, 2001). Thus, it is becoming more and more common for multiple generations of family members to live under one roof – and co-residence is not always easy (e.g., see Postigo & Honrubia, 2010, for findings related to co-residency challenges experienced by adult children). In other cases, a grandparent may be the sole caregiver for his or her grandchildren, a phenomenon that carries with it many challenges alongside the opportunities. A study conducted by Burton (1992), for example, discovered that primary caregiving grandparents (mostly grandmothers) received very little emotional support and reported high levels of depression, anxiety, and stress. Furthermore, it is not uncommon for adult children to participate in the care of their parents (an average of 65 million Americans provide care for an elderly parent; National Family Caregivers

Association, 2010), but what happens when an adult child must become the *sole* provider for a parent? Kleban, Brody, Schoonover, and Hoffman (1989) conducted a study on husbands' perceptions of their wives' caregiving for the wives' elderly mother. The authors found that the husbands whose mother-in-law lived with them felt there was more interference in their lives (e.g., planning family vacations, time spent with wives and children). In all of these brief examples, we can see potential for dark family functioning. We contend that, because of their increasing numbers and the stress connected to them, the dark (and bright) communication processes of these understudied, multigenerational family forms are in need of further examination. Their complexity warrants careful, systematic study, for family scholars cannot assume that the experiences are comparable to more commonly studied family structures.

Another source of family stress that is particularly salient in today's world is that associated with life in a military family. Since we have faced a constant stream of deployments during the early 2000s, scholars have begun to examine the effects of deployments on military families and how families' communication perpetuates or calms the stresses involved with such deployment. One such study conducted by Sahlstein, Maguire, and Timmerman (2009) explored how wives handle the communication challenges associated with the deployment routine. Specifically, the researchers reported that the communication struggles associated with deployments began during the pre-deployment stage, as wives fielded difficult questions from children ("Will daddy ever come back?") and questioned whether their husbands would return changed men. Based on frequent practice missions and prolonged separation prior to the actual deployment overseas, military wives reported that their communication habits with their spouse had changed due to the separation. One specific communication issue that has been found to impact the family is the amount of self-disclosure between military wives and their deployed husbands. Sahlstein and colleagues (2009) noted that the "wives struggled with what and how much they wanted to know about their husbands' deployment, and in turn, contemplated what to discuss about their own experiences during the deployment" (p. 433).

Joseph and Afifi (2009) also found that wives were less likely to disclose on issues that would cause their husbands undue stress. However, this lack of disclosure had effects on the wives' own health. Thus, it appears that the lack of self-disclosure during and after deployment contributes to some dark family functioning. These studies are just beginning to capture the complexity of military family life and to understand its correlated darkness. This area is one in particular where we feel that family communication scholars can not only advance our theoretical understanding of stressful family environments but also contribute to the lives of real men and women who are struggling to maintain their families pre-, during, and post-deployment.

(Dark) technology and (dark) family communication. In her review of what we could expect from "families of the future," Galvin (2004) wrote: "The family of the future will encounter rapidly changing environments due to unprecedented technological change. Family members will be faced with new issues and interaction patterns by technological changes in areas such as telecommunication, medical treatment, and education" (p. 676). Consider the technological advances we have seen over the eight years since Galvin's writing. Now, we own cell phones with the capability to snap photos, surf the web, and play movies. We "tweet" timely bits of information in an instant, while also keeping close watch on the happenings of our favorite celebrities or organizations. Finally, we upload, view, and share video clips with family and friends . . . and millions of others across the globe. Naturally, such inventions impact the way we communicate, and more specifically, the way we communicate with our families.

Evidence suggests that the influence of technology on our family communication is not always "bright." One older study revealed that fathers' home-computing time correlated positively with father-reported spousal conflict (Bird, Goss, & Bird, 1990), while more recent research indicated that wives expressed great dissatisfaction with their husbands' frequent computer usage (Morrison & Krugman, 2001). Another study monitored a group of parents and teenagers over their first two years of internet use (Kraut, Mukophadyay, Szczypula, Kiesler, & Scherlis, 2000). These scholars found that both the parents and teens used the internet to communicate with non-family members, and they spent less time communicating with family members than they had before they got the internet. Another study also discovered that an increase in cell phone usage correlated positively with distress and family dissatisfaction (Chelsey, 2005). Moreover, a report from the Pew Internet & American Life Project (2008) noted that while families use cell phones and the internet to stay connected and updated, those with multiple communication devices in the home are less likely to eat meals together and report less family satisfaction and family leisure time.

These are just a few ways in which we have seen the development of new technologies affect family functioning and communicative interactions (e.g., spending time together), and we do not anticipate a lull in technological changes. With so many technological advances every year, communication researchers have the opportunity to explore the benefits and downfalls of these changes. Interestingly, the examples above focus on how technology affects the nuclear "intact" family, often comprised of a father, mother, and children. This common tendency to privilege one family type in research over the other segues us into another research area we believe is in need of examination.

Broadening family ideologies. Most research in family communication, and, consequently, in dark family communication studies, still focuses on the nuclear family. One potential problem with this (among others) is that some family research is shaded darkly simply because certain families and family phenomena deemed as "normal" populate the family literature. Recall from the Darkness Model that dark message meanings are constructed by those experiencing the dark interaction, but also by those *observing* the interaction. As such, it is crucial that communication scholars widen their lens through which to view and observe family interactions to allow for more diverse analyses. Granted, some scholars and scholarship outlets are taking action to critique and question popular family ideologies (e.g., Coontz, 2003; Galvin, 2004). In fact, one of the foundational journals in family studies, the *Journal of Marriage and the Family*, dropped the *The* from the journal's title to illustrate this exact point.

Complete social acceptance of post-modern families has not occurred. One way we can see the limited acceptance and total ideological shift is the lack of a language to adequately describe these alternative family forms. As communication scholars, we know the reflective and constitutive role that language plays in the creation of our social realities. The lack of adequate language to capture diverse family forms "reflects" an invisibility, a non-normative existence. It is not too difficult, then, to make the inferential leap from invisible to dark, for what we do not know or cannot see is often feared or even reviled. The language that does exist constitutes a narrow range of acceptable, knowable (thus bright?) family forms; conversely, no adequate language exists for post-modern familial arrangements, thereby perpetuating their delegitimization.

However, we believe that Galvin (2006) has given us an important lexicon for beginning to symbolically and pragmatically recognize diverse family forms. In Dr. Galvin's words, "as families become increasingly diverse, *their definitional processes expand exponentially, rendering their identity highly discourse dependent*" (p. 3). She further explains, "families formed wholly or partly without biological and/or legal ties depend heavily on discourse processes to create their 'stickiness,' or bonding, to provide members with an internal sense of identity was well as an identity presented to outsiders" (p. 9). We argue, along with family scholars such as Galvin, that more attention needs to be paid to these discourse-dependent families and the communication processes (both bright and dark) that construct them as well as embody them. As noted above, discourse-dependent families come in many forms. For example, street families are groups of homeless youth who left their homes for various reasons, finding others who provided emotional and material support and companionship (Smith, 2008). One study found that homeless youth who create fictive kin relationships consider these relationships to possess a great source of social capital (McCarthy, Hagan, & Martin, 2002). One important outcome of this social capital includes protection. This study found that fictive street families keep youth out of violent situations more than other associations. We believe the field of family communication would benefit from more studies on fictive kin that include an examination of both the dark and bright aspects of having these relationships.

It is important to underscore that the variety of discourse-dependent family forms in and of themselves are not dark, nor are their inherent characteristics. But, with a language that legitimizes their existence, we can now study such discourse-dependent family forms in their entirety – bright, dark, and everything in between.

At this point, you may be particularly drawn to one or two of these research questions. Maybe you have even formulated your own question about a topic unrelated to those mentioned. Often, not all of the questions that we ask are best answered through the same method. Thus, it is important to select a method suitable for your particular question and subsequent investigation.

Methodological Choices When Studying Dark Family Communication

In addition to suggesting future ideas for research on the dark side of family life, we would like to present an overview of different ways one might question and conduct research on the topic. By no means is the review exhaustive. Also, we focus more on methods associated with the study types (i.e., quantitative, qualitative, or critical), rather than the underlying assumptions of particular paradigms.

Quantitative studies. Quantitative investigations dominate much of the family communication literature. In fact, when Stamp (2004) reviewed published family communication research, he found that approximately 90 percent of the journal articles used quantitative methods. Quantitative studies allow researchers to show how one thing (or, variable) relates to another, or differences between groups. Sometimes quantitative studies are descriptive, using methods such as surveys to obtain data. However, more complex studies incorporating experimental design (e.g., measuring subjects before and after a treatment) show causality (i.e., how one variable directly causes a certain effect). Importantly, outcomes from quantitative research can help us make predictions that scholars can generalize to other populations – which can lead to more positive outcomes for numerous families beyond the ones we study. John Gottman, a social psychologist and marital therapist, is a prime example of someone who uses quantitative methods to study the dark aspects of family communication. By assigning numerical codes to couples' conversations (e.g., speech content, facial expressions, voice intonation), Gottman successfully predicts divorce with over 90 percent accuracy (see Gottman, 1993). Additionally, from the multitude of divorce studies, Gottman and colleagues identified the communication behaviors of *successful* couples (e.g., using positive affect in everyday conversations; Gottman & Levenson, 2000).

More advanced statistical analyses and models (e.g., structural equation modeling) are becoming more common in family communication studies. Some advantages to using such models include, but are not limited to, the ability (a) to analyze dyadic and family level data, (b) to observe how variables affect multiple outcome variables, and (c) to test latent variable constructs. Researchers have utilized advanced statistical modeling to better understand darker family communication issues, such as parent–child conflict (Kashy, Donnellan, Burt, & McGue, 2008), (lack of) family well-being and physical health (Baiocchi-Wagner, 2010b; Koesten, Schrodt, & Ford, 2009), the chilling effect's impact on concealing family secrets (Afifi & Olson, 2005), and marital dissatisfaction (Weigel & Ballard-Reisch, 2008).

Consider the types of quantitative studies that could be developed using the Darkness Model. Future studies could include a survey study distributed to adult children who grew up in foster care. Questions on the survey could ask about their dark and bright experiences in order to learn more about the shades of darkness in this unique family form. This type of study could use the Darkness Model to examine the individual's reaction, how dyads within the family functioned as well as how this family form functioned, and how the adult foster children dealt with societal stereotypes and stigmas associated with the foster family form. Because one of the main components of the Darkness Model is the use of time, future studies should attempt to follow dark messages and processes longitudinally. For example, researchers could study the variable of addiction, such as alcoholism, and examine the impact of the disease on message construction and processing as well as dyadic and whole family functioning.

Qualitative studies. Sometimes scholars desire to get past the "big picture" typically provided by quantitative method designs. Instead of asking questions like, "How does A influence B?" or "Do A, B, and C, cause D?" scholars selecting qualitative methods usually hope to answer questions like, "How do families communicate about A?" or "How do family members experience B together?" As such, qualitative methods – observation, interviews, focus groups, respondent diary entries – allow scholars to (a) learn more about an *individual's* experience and meaning-making process and thus, (b) gain a more in-depth understanding of the situation and context (see Creswell, 2007). There are a variety of qualitative methodologies, which include, for example, grounded theory, case study, ethnography, narrative, and phenomenology (Creswell, 2007). Grounded theory allows a researcher the opportunity to create a theory for the specific phenomenon they are exploring. Case studies explore a specific occurrence or event and the communication that has occurred. Ethnography allows a researcher to study a culture and learn the intricacies in order to analyze the communication within that culture. Using a narrative approach for a study allows the researcher to hear the stories of the participants and analyze those stories to better understand how narratives function as a way of telling and knowing about one's world. Finally, phenomenology seeks to better understand the experiences of the participants and the communication that occurs within their experiences (Creswell, 2007). Both bright and dark communication can be explored using these qualitative methods.

Olson's (2002) work provides an example of qualitative methods in dark family communication studies. Olson explored a unique phenomenon – common-couple abuse – by conducting in-depth interviews with thirty-one individuals who experienced aggressive conflict with their partner. Each interview was recorded and transcribed. Then, by comparing and contrasting data from each interview (see Glaser & Strauss, 1967), Olson discovered that *multiple* forms of violent couples existed, contrary to the more simplistic, narrowed view of aggression drawn from earlier studies. In addition, Smith (2008) utilized two of the qualitative methods mentioned above. First, she conducted thirty interviews with homeless youth in order to capture their stories and experiences. Moreover in order to get at the heart of street families, Smith's second part consisted of ethnographic, or field, research. Smith used her connections through her outreach work and spent time visiting sites where homeless youth engaged in street activities. Smith found that while these street families are able to support most of the needs these youths are seeking, there are still dark aspects associated with being a member of this family, especially for females. One other example of qualitative family analysis is that of Canary (2008), who sought to understand how families that included a member with disabilities, used communication to construct "normal" identities. To uncover how individuals constructed their identities, Canary used a narrative view of identity and included interviews and observations of children with disabilities and their multiple family members as her primary methods of data collection. In doing so, Canary demonstrated how families' interactions within the family system and with outsiders contributed to an ongoing negotiation of contradictions.

With an array of choices available to design and conduct a qualitative study, the approach to studying the Darkness Model using these methods is vast. Other possible research ideas might include a grounded theory approach to understanding the process family members use in confronting another family member who has an addiction or illness. A phenomenological approach could be used to understand what it means to be a member of a religious sect that, to outsiders, more closely resembles a cult. The possibilities of research ideas are endless with qualitative research methods; what we have provided is just the beginning.

Critical studies. Critical studies are gaining momentum in family communication journals, thanks to feminist (see Allen, Lloyd, &

Few, 2009) and relational dialectics (Baxter, 2011) scholars, but still remain the most underrepresented in the subfield (Stamp, 2004). In addition to the qualitative methods already described, critical studies also use texts as data. Often, when we think of "texts," we immediately think of readable texts (e.g., books or magazines). However, the term *texts* can also refer to other forms, such as written interviews, observations, movies, or web sites. Critical studies tend to differ from most other qualitative studies, however, in that they seek to emancipate others (i.e., release or help free from a difficult situation).

Although critical investigations often use methods such as family member interviews or observation for data, one increasingly popular area for critical scholars is that of family policy and other issues associated with work–life balance. For example, organizational policies on maternity/paternity leave, childcare options, and welfare-to-work reform often dictate and/or redirect our thinking about family and associated responsibilities (e.g., Medved & Graham, 2006; Meisenbach, Remke, Buzzanell, & Liu, 2008; Perry-Jenkins, Pierce, & Goldberg, 2004; Zimmerman, Haddock, Current, & Ziemba, 2003).

In one highly cooperative study, eight authors from the University of Missouri jointly wrote about the ups and downs of mixing family life with academic life following a semester in which four faculty members (of the eleven in the department) were pregnant (Aubrey et al., 2008). Multiple views on the event (e.g., from those authors with children versus those without), compiled from transcripts of earlier recorded conversations, identified many of the tensions involved in work–life balance, including unclear and ineffectively communicated institutional policies, taxing professor–student relationships, and the stress of balancing research and teaching loads. Aubrey and colleagues suggested that for those in similar circumstances, having an open dialogue about work-life balance with colleagues is crucial, and that "policies must be written, visible, and the organization and its members must actively work to construct cultures that support the use of such policies" (p. 195).

Hopefully these examples give you an idea of how a dark family communication topic could be framed differently, depending upon the methodological approach assumed. Having knowledge about these research methods is useful, but the question becomes, how do you choose which type is best for your study?

How to choose? No method is "best." Rather, your choice to use quantitative, qualitative, or critical methods to investigate dark family communication phenomena is first, a reflection of the question you pose about dark family communication, and second, a reflection of how you view reality and how you believe you "come to know what you know" (see Anderson, 1996 for a discussion on epistemological foundations). In fact, we believe that the study of dark family communication is a complex phenomenon and is best understood through a combination of methods (see also Noller & Feeney, 2004). That is one reason we created the Darkness Model the way we did – it allows scholars to examine aspects of dark family communication by using quantitative methods, qualitative methods, and/or a critical approach, if they so choose. For example, maybe you want to know more about communication between older adult parents and their adult children. One of your research questions may be, "How do older adult parents experience living arrangement decisions being made by their adult children?" For this research question, you could complete a phenomenology, using interviews as your method. You might interview, for example, the older adult parents to understand their experiences of aging, loss of agency, and how these changes affect their self-perceptions. Another one of your research questions could be, "How do decisions of living arrangements for older adult parents, made by adult children, affect older adult parents' perceptions of self?" Parents could complete a questionnaire. Data obtained could be assessed for relationships and differences between the variables via various statistical analyses. Or, perhaps both of these questions interest you and a mixed methods approach best suits your needs.

As these examples demonstrate, multiple methodological choices abound. There is no one right way to study the dark side of family life; instead, we encourage a multiple methods approach, in general, and advocate for more critical scholarship, in particular.

Closing Words

With a variety of topic proposals and methodological suggestions made, we would be remiss if we ended this book without acknowledging the inherent difficulty in studying dark family encounters. The topic is not for everybody, and we have found this to be true in our own lives. For some, the subject matter is far too emotionally exhausting and personally troublesome to devote professional energies. Some individuals know this at the onset, thereby refusing to become a team member, while others only realize it after they begin a dark family-oriented research project and find they need to excuse themselves. Certainly, such patterns do not always happen, but we have learned through personal experience that studying the dark side of family communication indeed can be emotionally taxing. Thus, we encourage individuals to be very thoughtful and reflexive about choosing to study such subject matter.

If a person does have the intellectual and emotional grit, however, we believe the rewards far outweigh the costs. In our opinion, the more we can learn about family dysfunction, the more we can find ways to help families interact in healthier ways. That potential is truly inspirational. Yet, with that said, because of the emotional labor involved in this subject matter (both for the researcher and the family), abidance by the highest of ethical standards is a must. Conducting ethical research is always important, no matter the subject; however, when exploring matters that are potentially so painful, shameful, or harmful, it is imperative that careful attention be paid to the vulnerability of our participants and to the securing of their informed consent. The sentiment contained in the statement, "researcher do no harm," takes on added meaning in such a context.

For those of you contemplating dark family communication scholarship, we would like to end this chapter where we began – with the Darkness Model. More specifically, we highlighted in this chapter a few future areas of research that need further study and several different methodological approaches to the study of dark family communication. Moreover, processes involved in the families' prominent use of technology, for instance, offer dark family scholars new terrain for study. We contend that the Darkness Model provides a much needed theoretical framework for uncovering dynamics involved in the darker side of family life. Following our model's components, we leave you with a set of questions to ask yourself as you begin to consider dark family communication processes:

"What makes this particular message 'dark'?" (Nature of dark communication)

"How is the dark message assigned meaning by family members? Is this meaning different for those experiencing it versus those observing the message?" (Meaning-making processes)

"What impact does the message produce at the individual, dyadic, familial, and societal levels?" (Four interlocking levels). How do these levels influence the meaning assigned to a message?

"What do dark messages and their outcomes look like over time?" (Synchronic vs. diachronic time issues)

Of course, these are just examples; certainly there are many other questions researchers could ask to guide their inquiries. We offer these as a springboard for your ideas and invite you into the Moore family household for one final discussion of dark family communication.

Case Study

Lucy bolted straight up, her hair mangled from the few hours of sleep she managed to get in. She sat there, stunned, trying to shake the feeling, that eerie feeling. Bobby, who slipped into her room in the middle of the night, slept soundly at the foot of her bed. Freddie knocked lightly on her door before entering the room, with a disheveled Steve following behind.

"I avoided dad when we got home last night," Freddie informed Lucy.

"Yeah, man, it felt like we were walking into jail cells last night," Steve chimed in, noting his metaphor of this house being a jail and the kids feeling like prisoners.

"I called mom out on her drinking," Lucy said. "She was pretty cool. I honestly think she is going to get help. Bobby," who slowly began to wake at the sound of his name, "asked about them divorcing."

Freddie tossed Bobby's hair and then sat at his feet. Steve grabbed the chair at Lucy's desk. Freddie took in a deep breath and as he slowly exhaled "I've decided to tell dad I'm gay."

In their parents' room, Janice and Fred awoke and sat on the bed. "Lucy knows about my drinking. I did some research and decided to go to AA and suggest that Lucy and Freddie go to Al-Anon."

Fred sat there in silence.

"I am the one to blame here. My drinking is the foundation of the problem between you and Freddie. I want to fix it."

"Your drinking is not to blame. Yes, it is a problem but not the problem between me and Freddie," Fred replied. "I want him to have more than I did."

"But Freddie is not you or Brian. He's Freddie. You need to see that. You need to accept that."

Silence filled the room again.

"Kids," Fred said as he entered the kitchen, the children including Freddie and Steve already at the breakfast table eating Coco Puffs and leftover apple turnovers.

"Dad."

"Mr Moore."

"We need to talk about . . ."

Freddie interrupted. "Dad I'm gay, and I do not want to join the military."

Janice smiled at her son, overwhelmed with pride for him as he told his father the truth. She became caught up in the moment. "Children, Fred, mom, I'm an alcoholic."

The room, once again, filled with silence.

Discussion Questions

1. Explain what is happening in the Moore situation by using the Darkness Model.
2. How do the interlocking structures influence the meaning making being assigned to what is being said?
3. You are one of the Moores. What happens next?

For Further Thought and Discussion

Theoretical Considerations

1. Consider each level of the Dark Side of Family Communication Model. Which aspects most interest you? What particular dark side family communication phenomena would you want to investigate?

Methodological Considerations

1. Using your response from the previous question, what might your research question look like if you employed one or more quantitative methods? Qualitative methods? A critical approach?
2. What ethical issues do you feel are particularly relevant to the study of dark family communication? What are some specific factors that researchers need to consider as they enact ethical dark side family scholarship?

Practical Considerations

1. Consider how technological advancements have affected your life. What aspects of your technological use with your family members are bright? Dark? Gray?
2. What personal concerns do you have about conducting dark family communication? How can dark side researchers resist becoming desensitized to the darker side of human existence? What recommendations would you make to someone before he/she decided to study some dark family process?

References

Afifi, T. D., McManus, T., Steuber, K., & Coho, A. (2009). Verbal avoidance and dissatisfaction in intimate conflict situations. *Human Communication Research, 35,* 357–383.

Afifi, T. D., & Olson, L. N. (2005). The chilling effect in families and the pressure to conceal secrets. *Communication Monographs, 72,* 192–216.

Afifi, T. D., Olson, L. N., & Armstrong, C. (2005). The chilling effect and family secrets: Examining the role of self protection, other protection, and communication efficacy. *Human Communication Research, 31,* 564–598.

Afifi, T. D., & Steuber, K. (2009). The revelation risk model (RRM): Factors that predict the revelation of secrets and the strategies used to reveal them. *Communication Monographs, 76,* 144–176.

Afifi, W. A., & Caughlin, J. (2005). Examining the roles of self-esteem and identity concerns in decisions about, and consequences of, revealing secrets. Presented at International Communication Association, New York.

Afifi, W. A., & Caughlin, J. P. (2006). A close look at revealing secrets and some consequences that follow. *Communication Research, 33,* 467–488.

Ainsworth, M. D. S. (1969). Object relations, dependency, and attachment: A theoretical review of the infant-mother relationship. *Child Development, 40,* 969–1025.

Ainsworth, M. D. S., Blehar, M. C., Waters, E., & Wall, S. (1978). *Patterns of attachment: A psychological study of the strange situation.* Hillsdale, NJ: Lawrence Erlbaum.

Akintunde, D. O. (2010). Female genital mutilation: A socio-cultural gang up against womanhood. *Feminist Theology, 18,* 192–206.

Alberts, J. K. (1988). An analysis of couples' conversational complaints. *Communication Monographs, 55,* 184–197.

Allen, K., Fine, M., & Demo, D. (2000). An overview of family diversity: Controversies, questions, and values. In D. Demo, K. Allen, & M. Fine (eds), *Handbook of family diversity* (pp. 1–13). New York: Oxford University Press.

Allen, K., Lloyd, S., & Few, A. (2009). Reclaiming feminist theory, method and praxis for family studies. In S. Lloyd, A. Few, & K. Allen (eds), *Handbook of feminist family studies* (pp. 3–17). Los Angeles, CA: Sage.

American Academy of Pediatrics (2010). Policy statement – ritual genital cutting of female minors. *Pediatrics, 125*, 1088–1093.

American Psychiatric Association (2000). *Diagnostic and statistical manual of mental disorders* (4th edn, text revision) (DSM-IV-TR). Arlington, VA.

Andersen, P. A., & Guerrero, L. K. (1998). The bright side of relational communication: Interpersonal warmth as a social emotion. In P. A. Andersen & L. K. Guerrero (eds), *Handbook of communication and emotion* (pp. 303–329). San Diego, CA: Academic Press.

Anderson, A. C., & Dill, K. E. (2000). Video games and aggressive thoughts, feelings, and behavior in the laboratory and in life. *Journal of Personality and Social Psychology, 78*, 772–790.

Anderson, J. A. (1996). *Communication theory: Epistemological foundations.* New York: Guilford Press.

Anderson, K. L., Umberson, D., & Elliott, S. (2004). Violence and abuse in families. In A. L. Vangelisti (ed.), *Handbook of family communication* (pp. 609–628). Mahwah, NJ: Lawrence Erlbaum.

Arrington, M. I. (2005). "She's right behind me all the way": An analysis of prostate cancer narratives and changes in family relationship. *Journal of Family Communication, 5*, 141–162.

Asada, K. J. K., Lee, E., Levine, T. R., & Ferrara, M. H. (2004). Narcissism and empathy as predictors of obsessive relational intrusion. *Communication Research Reports, 21*, 379–390.

Aubrey, J. S., Click, M., Dougherty, D., Fine, M., Kramer, M., Meisenbach, R., et al. (2008). We do babies! The trials, tribulations, and triumphs of pregnancy and parenting in the academy. *Women's Studies in Communication, 31*, 186–195.

Aune, K., & Comstock, J. (2002). An exploratory investigation of jealousy in the family. *Journal of Family Communication, 2*, 29–39.

Azadarmaki, T. (2008). Television, religious media, and the mirror relationship between family, government, and religion in Iran. *Journal of Media and Religion, 7*, 45–55.

Baiocchi, E., Mbure, W. G., Wilson-Kratzer, J. M., Olson, L. N., & Symonds, S. (2009). Shedding "light": A dark side of family communication model. A paper presented at National Communication Association, Chicago, IL.

Baiocchi-Wagner, E. (2010a). Hate in the family system? Manuscript in progress.

Baiocchi-Wagner, E. (2010b) "The role of family communication in individual attitudes and behaviors concerning nutrition and physical activity." Diss. University of Missouri. Print.

Baker, E., Sanchez, L., Nock, S., & Wright, J. (2009). Covenant marriage and the sanctification of gendered marital roles. *Journal of Family Issues, 30*, 147–178.

References

Ballard-Reisch, S. D., & Weigel, D. J. (2006). Established and promising models of family communication research. In L. H. Turner & R. West (eds), *The family communication sourcebook* (pp. 61–82). Thousand Oaks , CA: Sage.

Barbee, A. P., Rowatt, T. L., & Cunningham, M. R. (1998). When a friend is in need: Feelings about seeking, giving, and receiving social support. In P. A. Andersen & L. K. Guerrero (eds), *Handbook of communication and emotion* (pp. 281–301). San Diego, CA: Academic Press.

Barkun, M. (1997). *Religion and the racist right: The origins of the Christian Identity movement* (revised edn). Chapel Hill, NC: University of North Carolina Press.

Barnett, O., Miller-Perrin, C. L., & Perrin, R. D. (2005). *Family violence across the lifespan: An introduction* (2nd edn). Thousand Oaks, CA: Sage.

Bartholomew, K., & Horowitz, L. M. (1991). Attachment styles among young adults: A test of a four-category model. *Journal of Personality and Social Psychology, 61*, 226–244.

Baumeister, R., Bushman, B., & Campbell, W. (2000). Self-esteem, narcissism, and aggression: Does violence result from low self-esteem or from threatened egotism? *Current Directions in Psychological Science, 9*, 26–29.

Baumrind, D. (1971). Current patterns of parental authority. *Developmental Psychology Monographs, 4*, 1–103.

Baumrind, D. (1996). The discipline controversy revisited. *Family Relations, 45*, 405–411.

Baxter, L. A. (2011). *Voicing relationships: A dialogic perspective*. Los Angeles, CA: Sage.

Baxter, L. A., & Braithwaite, D. O. (2006a). Family rituals. In L. H. Turner & R. West (eds), *The family communication sourcebook* (pp. 259–280). Thousand Oaks, CA: Sage.

Baxter, L. A. & Braithwaite, D. (2006b). Metatheory and theory in family communication research. In D. Braithwaite & L. Baxter (eds), *Engaging theories in family communication: Multiple perspectives* (pp. 1–15). Thousand Oaks, CA: Sage.

Baxter, L. A., & Braithwaite, D. O. (eds). (2008). *Engaging theories in interpersonal communication: Multiple perspectives*. Thousand Oaks, CA: Sage.

Beatty, M. J., McCroskey, J. C., & Valenic, K. M. (2001). *The biology of communication: A communibiological perspective*. Cresskill, NJ: Hampton Press.

Beck, A. R., & Alford, B. A. (2009). *Depression: Causes and treatment* (2nd edn). Philadelphia, PA: University of Pennsylvania Press.

Becker, T. E., Billings, R. S., Eveleth, D. M., & Gilbert, N. W. (1997). Validity scores on three attachment style scales: Exploratory and confirmatory evidence. *Educational and Psychological Measurement, 57*, 477–493.

Bedford, V. H., & Blieszner, R. (1997). Personal relationships in later life families. In S. Duck (ed.), *Handbook of personal relationships* (2nd edn, pp. 523–539). New York: Wiley.

Benet-Martinez, V., & Haritatos, J. (2005). Bicultural Identity Integration (BII): Components and psychosocial antecedents. *Journal of Personality 73*, 1015–1050.

Berkowitz, L. (1998). Aggressive personalities. In D. Barone, F. Hersen, & V. Van Hasselt (eds), *Advanced personality* (pp. 263–285). New York: Plenum Press.

Berns, S. B., Jacobson, N. S., & Gottman, J. M. (1999). Demand/withdraw interaction patterns between different types of batterers and their spouses. *Journal of Marital and Family Therapy, 25(3)*, 337–348.

Bird, G., Goss, R., & Bird, G. W. (1990). Effects of home computer use on fathers' lives. *Family Relations, 39*, 438–442.

Bok, S. (1983). *Secrets: On the ethics of concealment and revelation.* New York: Vintage Books.

Bonilla-Silva, E. (2006). *Racism without racists: Color-blind racism and the persistence of racial inequality in the United States* (2nd edn). Lanham, MD: Rowman & Littlefield.

Booth, A., Crouter, A. C., & Clements, M. (2001). *Couples in conflict.* Mahwah, NJ: Lawrence Erlbaum Associates.

Booth-Butterfield, M., & Sidelinger, R. (1998). The influence of family communication on the college-aged child: Openness, attitudes, and actions about sex and alcohol. *Communication Quarterly, 46*, 295–308.

Boss, P. (1988). *Family stress management.* Newbury Park, CA: Sage.

Boss, P. (2002). *Family stress management: A contextual approach* (2nd edn). Thousand Oaks, CA: Sage.

Botta, R. A., & Dumlao, R. (2002). How do conflict and communication patterns between fathers and daughters contribute to or offset eating disorders? *Health Communication, 14*, 199–219.

Botwin, M. D., Buss, D. M., & Shackelford, T. K. (1997). Personality and mate preference: Five factors in mate selection and marital satisfaction. *Journal of Personality, 65*, 107–136.

Bowlby, J. (1969/1982). *Attachment and loss: Vol I. Attachment* (2nd edn). New York: Basic Books.

Bowlby, J. (1973). *Attachment and loss: Vol. II. Separation: Anxiety and anger.* New York: Basic Books.

Bowlby, J. (1977). The making and breaking of affectional bonds. *British Journal of Psychiatry, 130*, 201–210.

Bowlby, J. (1979). *The making and breaking of affectional bonds.* London: Tavistock Publications.

Bowlby, J. (1980). *Attachment and loss: Vol. III. Loss: Sadness and depression.* New York: Basic Books.

Bradford, L., & Petronio, S. (1998). Strategic embarrassment: The culprit of emotion. In P. A. Andersen & L. K. Guerrero (eds), *Handbook of communication and emotion* (pp. 99–121). San Diego, CA: Academic Press.

References

Braithwaite, D. O., & Baxter, L. A. (2006). *Engaging theories in family communication: Multiple perspectives.* Thousand Oaks, CA: Sage.

Branje, S. J. T., van Lieshout, C. F. M., & van Aken, M. A. G. (2004). Relations between Big Five personality characteristics and perceived support in adolescents' families. *Journal of Personality and Social Psychology, 86,* 615–628.

Brownridge, D. A. (2010). Does the situational couple violence-intimate terrorism typology explain cohabitors' high risk of intimate partner violence? *Journal of Interpersonal Violence, 25,* 1264–1283.

Burleson, B. R., & Goldsmith, D. J. (1998). How the comforting process works: Alleviating emotional distress through conversationally induced reappraisals. In P. A. Andersen & L. K. Guerrero (eds), *Handbook of communication and emotion* (pp. 245–280). San Diego, CA: Academic Press.

Burleson, B., & Kunkel, A. (2002). Parental and peer contribution to the emotional support skills of the child: From whom do children learn to express support? *Journal of Family Communication, 2,* 79–97.

Burton, L. (1992). Black grandparents rearing children of drug-addicted parents: Stressors, outcomes and social service needs. *The Gerontologist, 32,* 744–751.

Busby, D. M., & Holman, T. B. (2009). Perceived match or mismatch on the Gottman conflict styles: Associations with relationship outcome variables. *Family Process, 48,* 531–545.

Button, D. M., & Gealt, R. (2010). High risk behaviors among victims of sibling violence. *Journal of Family Violence, 25,* 131–140.

Cahn, D. D. (2009). An evolving communication perspective on family violence. In D. D. Cahn (ed.), *Family violence: Communication processes* (pp. 1–24). Albany, NY: SUNY Press.

Cai, D. A., & Fink, E. L. (2002). Conflict style differences between individualists and collectivists. *Communication Monographs, 69,* 67–87.

Campbell, W. K. (1999). Narcissism and romantic attraction. *Journal of Personality and Social Psychology, 77,* 1254–1270.

Canary, D. J., Spitzberg, B. H., & Semic, B. A. (1998). The experience and expression of anger in interpersonal settings. In P. A. Andersen & L. K. Guerrero (eds), *Handbook of communication and emotion* (pp. 189–213). San Diego, CA: Academic Press.

Canary, H. (2008). Negotiating dis/ability in families: Constructions and contradictions. *Journal of Applied Communication Research, 36,* 437–458.

Cann, A., & Calhoun, L. G. (2001). Perceived personality associations with differences in sense of humor: Stereotypes of hypothetical others with high or low senses of humor. *Humor: International Journal of Humor Research, 14,* 117–130.

Carnes, P. J. (1989). Sexually addicted families: Clinical use of the Circumplex model. In D. H. Olson, C. S. Russell, & D. H. Sprenkle (eds., *Circumplex model: Systemic assessment and treatment of families* (pp. 112–140). Binghamton, NY: Haworth Press.

Carroll, J. (2007). Most Americans approve of interracial marriages. Retrieved April 22, 2010 from Gallup News Service http://www.gallup.com/poll/28417/most-americans-approve-interracial-marriages.aspx

Caughlin, J. P., & Huston, T. L. (2002). A contextual analysis of the association between demand/withdraw and marital satisfaction. *Personal Relationships, 9,* 95–119.

Caughlin, J. P. & Petronio, S. (2004). Privacy in families. In A. L. Vangelisti (ed.), *Handbook of Family Communication* (pp. 379–412). Mahwah, NJ: Lawrence Erlbaum Associates.

Caughlin, J. P. & Vangelisti, A. L. (1999). Desire for change in one's partner as a predictor of the demand/withdraw pattern of marital communication. *Communication Monographs, 66,* 66–89.

Chao, M.-R. (2011). Family interaction relationship types and differences in parent–child interactions. *Social Behavior and Personality, 39,* 897–914. doi: 10.2224/sbp.2011.39.7.897.

Chelsey, N. (2005). Blurring boundaries? Linking technology use, spillover, individual distress, and family satisfaction. *Journal of Marriage and Family, 67,* 1237–1248.

Chen, F., Short, S., & Entwisle, B. (2000). The impact of grandparental proximity on maternal child care in China. *Population Research and Policy Review, 19,* 571–590.

Childhelp (2010). *National child abuse statistics.* Retrieved September 29, 2010 from http://www.childhelp.org/pages/statistics

Christensen, A., & Shenk, J. L. (1991). Communication, conflict, and psychological distance in nondistressed, clinical, and divorcing couples. *Journal of Consulting and Clinical Psychology, 59,* 458–463.

Christiano, K. (2000). Religion and the family in modern American culture. In S. K. Houseknecht & J. G. Pankhurst (eds), *Family, religion, and social change in diverse societies* (pp. 43–78). Oxford: Oxford University Press.

Christie, R., & Geis, F. L. (1970). *Studies in Machiavellianism.* New York: Academic Press.

Christopoulos, C., Bonvillian, J. D., & Crittenden, P. M. (1988). Maternal language input and child maltreatment. *Infant Mental Health Journal, 9,* 272–286.

Clancy, S. M., & Dollinger, S. J. (1993). Identity, self, and personality: I. Identity status and the Five Factor model of personality. *Journal of Research on Adolescence, 3,* 227–245.

Clarke, M., & Hornick, J. (1984). The development of the nurturance inventory: An instrument for assessing parenting practices. *Child Psychiatry & Human Development, 15,* 49–63.

Claxton-Oldfield, S., & Butler, B. (1998). Portrayal of stepparents in movie plot summaries. *Psychological Reports, 82,* 879–882.

Coleman, M., Ganong, L., & Fine, M. A. (2004). Communication in step-

References

families. In A. Vangelisti (ed.), *Handbook of family communication* (pp. 215–232). Mahwah, NJ: Lawrence Erlbaum.

Collins, N. L., & Read, S. J. (1990). Adult attachment, working models, and relationship quality in dating couples. *Journal of Personality and Social Psychology, 58,* 644–663.

Collins, R. (1981). *Sociology since midcentury: Essays in theory cumulation.* New York: Academic Press.

Conquering Stressful Family Hurdles (2010, September 1). [Quotes about family problems]. Retrieved from http://www.conquering-stressful-family-hurdles.com/

Coontz, S. (2000). Historical perspectives on family diversity. In D. H. Demo, K. R. Allen, & M. A. Fine (eds), *Handbook of family diversity* (pp. 15–31). New York: Oxford University Press.

Coontz, S. (2003). Diversity and communication values in the family. *Journal of Family Communication, 3,* 187–192.

Cornwall, M. (1988). The influence of three agents of religious socialization: Family, church, and peers. In D. Thomas (ed.), *The religion and family connection: Social science perspectives* (pp. 207–231). Provo, UT: Religious Studies Center, Brigham Young University.

Costa, P. T., Jr., & McCrae, R. R. (1988). From catalog to classification: Murray's needs and the five-factor model. *Journal of Personality and Social Psychology, 55,* 258–265.

Cramer, D. (1993). Personality and marital dissolution. *Personality and Individual Differences, 14,* 605–607.

Creswell, J. W. (2007). *Qualitative inquiry and research design: Choosing among five approaches* (2nd edn). Thousand Oaks, CA: Sage.

Cupach, W. R., & Olson, L. N. (2006). Emotion regulation theory: A lens for viewing family conflict and violence. In D. Braithwaite & L. Baxter (eds), *Engaging theories in family communication: Multiple perspectives* (pp. 213–228). Thousand Oaks, CA: Sage.

Cuperman, R., & Ickes, W. (2009). Big Five predictors of behavior and perceptions in initial dyadic interactions: Personality similarity helps extraverts and introverts, but hurts "disagreeables." *Journal of Personality and Social Psychology, 97,* 6, 7–684.

Daly, J. A. (2002). Personality and interpersonal communication. In M. L. Knapp & J. A. Daly (eds), *Handbook of Interpersonal Communication* (3rd edn, pp. 133–180). Thousand Oaks, CA: Sage.

Davidson, J., & Widman, T. (2002). The effect of group size on interfaith marriage among Catholics. *Journal for the Scientific Study of Religion, 41,* 397–404.

Davis, S., & Pearce, L. (2007). Adolescents' work-family gender ideologies and educational expectations. *Sociological Perspectives, 50,* 249–271.

Deater-Deckard, K., Dodge, K., Bates, J., & Pettit, G. (1996). Physical discipline among African American and European American mothers: Links to children's externalizing behaviors. *Developmental Psychology, 32,* 1065–1072.

Denzin, N. K. (1982). Notes on criminology and criminality. In H. E. Pepinsky (ed.), *Rethinking criminology* (pp. 115–130). Beverly Hills, CA: Sage.

Diggs, R., & Socha, T. (2004). Communication, families, and exploring the boundaries of cultural diversity. In A. Vangelisti (ed.), *Handbook of family communication* (pp. 249–266). Mahwah, NJ: Lawrence Erlbaum.

Dominguez, M. M., & Carton, J. S. (1997). The relationship between self-actualization and parenting style. *Journal of Social Behavior and Personality, 12,* 1093–1100.

Duck, S. (1994). Stratagems, spoils, and a serpent's tooth: On the delights and dilemmas of personal relationships. In W. R. Cupach & B. H. Spitzberg (eds), *The dark side of interpersonal communication* (pp. 3–21). Hillsdale, NJ: Lawrence Erlbaum.

Duck, S. (2011). *Rethinking relationships.* Los Angeles, CA: Sage.

Duggan, A. (2007). Sex differences in communicative attempts to curtail depression: An inconsistent nurturing as control perspective. *Western Journal of Communication, 71,* 114–135.

Duggan, A., Dailey, R., & Le Poire, B. (2008). Reinforcement and punishment of substance abuse during ongoing interactions: A conversational test of inconsistent nurturing as control theory. *Journal of Health Communication, 13,* 417–433.

Dunbar, N. E., & Burgoon, J. K. (2005). Perceptions of power and interactional dominance in interpersonal relationships. *Journal of Social and Personal Relationships, 22,* 207–233.

Duran, R. L., & Kelly, L. (1989). The cycle of shyness: A study of self-perceptions of communication performance. *Communication Reports, 2,* 30–38.

Dutton, D. G., & Bodnarchuk, M. (2005). Through a psychological lens. In D. R. Loseke, R. J. Gelles, & M. M. Cavanaugh (eds), *Current controversies on family violence* (2nd edn), pp. 5–18). Thousand Oaks, CA: Sage.

Eckstein, N. (2004). Emergent issues in families experiencing adolescent-to-parent abuse. *Western Journal of Communication, 68,* 365–388.

Eckstein, N. (2007). Adolescent-to-parent abuse: Exploring the communicative patterns leading to verbal, physical and emotional abuse. In B. Spitzberg & W. Cupach (eds), *The dark side of interpersonal communication* (2nd edn, pp. 363–388). Mahwah, NJ: Lawrence Erlbaum.

Ehrenberg, M. F., Hunter, M. A., & Elterman, M. F. (1996). Shared parenting agreements after marital separation: The roles of empathy and narcissism. *Journal of Consulting and Clinical Psychology, 64,* 808–818. doi: 10.1037/0022–006X.64.4.808

Ellis, A., & Abrams, M. (with Lidia D. Abrams) (2009). *Personality theories: Critical perspectives.* Los Angeles, CA: Sage.

References

Eriksen, S., & Jensen, V. (2006). All in the family? Family environmental factors in sibling violence. *Journal of Family Violence, 21,* 497–507.

Eysenck, H., & Eysenck, M. (1985). *Personality and individual differences: A natural science approach.* New York: Plenum.

Federal Investigative Bureau (1999, November). Project Megiddo. Retrieved April 22, 2010 from Center for Studies on New Religions http://www.cesnur. org/testi/FBI_006.htm#Anchor-III-43266

Feeney, J. A., & Noller, P. (1990). Attachment style as a predictor of adult romantic relationships. *Journal of Personality and Social Psychology, 58,* 281–291.

Feeney, J. A., & Noller, P. (1992). Attachment style and romantic love: Relationship dissolution. *Australian Journal of Psychology, 44,* 69–74.

Fitness, J., & Duffield, J. (2004). Emotion and communication in families. In A. L. Vangelisti (ed.), *Handbook of family communication* (pp. 473–494). Mahwah, NJ: Lawrence Erlbaum.

Fitzpatrick, M. A. (1988). *Between husbands and wives: Communication in marriage.* Newbury Park, CA: Sage.

Fitzpatrick, M., & Caughlin, J. P. (2002). Interpersonal communication in family relationships. In M. L. Knapp & J. A. Daly (eds), *Handbook of interpersonal communication* (pp. 726–777). Thousand Oaks, CA: Sage.

Floyd, K., Mikkelson, A. C., & Judd, J. (2006). Defining the family through relationships. In L. H. Turner & R. West (eds), *The family communication sourcebook* (pp. 21–39). Thousand Oaks, CA: Sage.

Floyd, K., & Morman, M. T. (2006). Introduction. In K. Floyd & M. T. Morman (eds), *Widening the family circle: New research in family communication* (pp. xi–xvi). Thousand Oaks, CA: Sage.

Foley, M. K., & Duck, S. (2006). "That dear octopus": A family-based model of intimacy. In L. H. Turner & R. West (eds), *The family communication sourcebook* (pp. 183–200). Thousand Oaks, CA: Sage.

Foucault, M. (1976). *The history of sexuality: Vol. 1. An introduction.* New York: Vintage.

Galvin, K. M. (2004). The family of the future: What do we face? In A. L. Vangelisti (ed.), *Handbook of family communication* (pp. 675–698). Mahwah, NJ: Lawrence Erlbaum.

Galvin, K. M. (2006). Diversity's impact on defining the family: Discourse-dependence and identity. In L. Turner & R. West (eds), *The family communication sourcebook* (pp. 3–19). Thousand Oaks, CA: Sage.

Galvin, K. M., Bylund, C. L. & Brommel, B. J. (2004). *Family communication: Cohesion and change.* New York: Longman.

Galvin, K. M., Dickson, F. C., & Marrow, S. R. (2006). Systems theory: Patterns of (w)holes in family communication. In D. O. Braithwaite & L. A. Baxter (eds), *Engaged theories in family communication: Multiple perspectives* (pp. 309–324). Thousand Oaks, CA: Sage.

References

Georgas, J., Mylonas, K., Bafiti, T., Poortinga,Y., Christakopoulou, S., Kagitcibasi, C., et al. (2001). Functional relationships in the nuclear and extended family: A 16-culture study. *International Journal of Psychology, 36,* 289–300.

Gerbner, G., Gross, L., Morgan, M., Signorielli, N., & Shanahan, J. (2002). Growing up with television: Cultivation processes. In J. Bryant & D. Zillmann (eds), *Media effects: Advances in theory and research* (2nd edn) (pp. 43–67). Mahwah, NJ: Lawrence Erlbaum.

Geronimi, C., Jackson, W., & Luske, H. (directors). (1950). *Cinderella* [animated movie]. USA: Walt Disney Productions.

Gershoff, E. T. (2002). Parental corporal punishment and associated child behaviors and experiences: A meta-analytic and theoretical review. *Psychological Bulletin, 128,* 539–579.

Giles, H., Noels, K. A., Williams, A., Ota, H., Lim, T. S., Ng, S., et al. (2003). Intergenerational communication across cultures: Young people's perceptions of conversations with family elders, non-family elders and same-age peers. *Journal of Cross-Cultural Gerontology, 18,* 1–32.

Glaser, B. G., & Strauss, A. L. (1967). *The discovery of grounded theory: Strategies for qualitative research.* New York: Aldine.

Gottman, J. M. (1993). The roles of conflict engagement, escalation, and avoidance in marital interaction: A longitudinal view of five types of couples. *Journal of Consulting and Clinical Psychology, 61,* 6–15.

Gottman, J. (1994). *What predicts divorce? The relationship between marital processes and marital outcomes.* Mahwah, NJ: Lawrence Erlbaum.

Gottman, J. M. & Carrera, S. (2000). Welcome to the love lab. *Psychology Today, 33,* 42–49.

Gottman, J. M., Jacobson, N. S., Rushe, R. H., Shortt, J. W., Babcock, J., La Taillade, J. J., & Waltz, J. (1995). The relationship between heart rate reactivity, emotionally aggressive behavior, and general violence in batterers. *Journal of Family Psychology, 9,* 227–248.

Gottman, J. M., Katz, L. F., & Hooven, C. (1997). *Meta-emotion: How families communicate emotionally.* Mahwah, NJ: Erlbaum.

Gottman, J. M., & Krokoff, L. J. (1989). Marital interaction and satisfaction: A longitudinal view. *Journal of Consulting and Clinical Psychology, 57,* 47–52.

Gottman, J., & Levenson, R. (2000). The timing of divorce: Predicting when a couple will divorce over a 14-year period. *Journal of Marriage and Family, 62,* 737–745.

Grams, W. C., & Rogers, R. W. (1989). Power and personality: Effects of Machiavellianism, need for approval, and motivation on use of influence tactics. *Journal of General Psychology, 117,* 71–82.

Great Inspirational Quotes (2010, September 1). [list of quotes]. Retrieved from http://www.great-inspirational-quotes.com/family-quotes.html

References

Greenberg, J. R., & Mitchell, S. A. (1983). *Object relations in psychoanalytic theory*. Cambridge, MA: Harvard University Press.

Grych, J. H., & Fincham, F. D. (1990). Marital conflict and children's adjustment: A cognitive-contextual framework. *Psychological Bulletin, 108,* 267–290.

Guerrero, L. K. (1996). Attachment-style differences in intimacy and involvement: A test of the four-category model. *Communication Monographs, 63,* 269–292.

Gunter, B., Harrison, J., & Wykes, M. (2003). *Violence on television: Distribution, form, context, and themes*. Erlbaum: Mahwah, NJ.

Hastings, S. O. (2000). Self-disclosure and identity management by bereaved parents. *Communication Studies, 51,* 352–371.

Hazan, C., & Shaver, P. (1987). Conceptualizing romantic love as an attachment process. *Journal of Personality and Social Psychology, 52,* 511–524.

Heavy, C. L., Christensen, A., & Malamuth, N. M. (1995). The longitudinal impact of demand and withdrawal during marital conflict. *Journal of Consulting and Clinical Psychology, 63,* 797–801.

Heavy, C. L., Layne, C., & Christensen, A. (1993). Gender and conflict structure in marital interaction: A replication and extension. *Journal of Consulting and Clinical Psychology, 61,* 16–27.

Heider, F. (1958). *The psychology of interpersonal relations*. New York: Riley.

Heisel, A., La France, B., & Beatty, M. (2003). Self-reported extraversion, neuroticism, and psychoticism as predictors of peer related verbal aggressiveness and affinity-seeking competence. *Communication Monographs, 70,* 1–15.

Holtzworth-Munroe, A., Meehan, J. C., Herron, K., Rehman, U., & Stuart, G. (2000). Testing the Holtzworth-Munroe and Stuart (1994) batterer typology. *Journal of Consulting and Clinical Psychology, 68,* 1000–1019.

Holtzworth-Munroe, A., Smutzler, N., & Stuart, G. L. (1998). Demand and withdraw communication among couples experiencing husband violence. *Journal of Consulting and Clinical Psychology, 66,* 731–743.

Holtzworth-Munroe, A., & Stuart, G. L. (1994). Typologies of male batterers: Three subtypes and the differences among them. *Psychological Bulletin, 116,* 476–497.

Horppu, R., & Ikonen-Varila, M. (2001). Are attachment styles general interpersonal orientations? Applicants' perceptions and emotions in interaction with evaluators in a college entrance examination. *Journal of Social and Personal Relationships, 18,* 131–148.

Hudak, J., Krestan, J. A., & Bepko, C. (2005). Alcohol problems and the family life cycle. In B. Carter & M. McGoldrick (eds), *The expanded family life cycle: Individual, family and social perspectives* (3rd edn, pp. 455–469). Boston, MA: Allyn & Bacon.

Infante, D. A., Chandler, T. A., & Rudd, J. E. (1989). Test of an argumentative skill deficiency model of interspousal violence. *Communication Monographs, 56,* 163–177.

References

Infante, D. A., Sabourin, T. C., Rudd, J. E., & Shannon, E. A. (1990). Verbal aggression in violent and nonviolent marital disputes. *Communication Quarterly, 38,* 361–371.

Infante, D. A., & Wigley, C. J. (1986). Verbal aggressiveness: An interpersonal model and measure. *Communication Monographs, 53,* 61–69.

Jackson, J. K. (1954/2002). The adjustment of the family to alcoholism. In E. Rubington & M. S. Weinberg (eds), *Deviance: The interactionist perspective* (8th edn, pp. 68–80). Boston, MA: Allyn and Bacon.

Jacobson, N. S., Gottman, J. M., Waltz, J., Rushe, R., Babcock, J., & Holtzworth-Munroe, A. (1994). Affect, verbal content, and psychophysiology and the argument of couples with a violent husband. *Journal of Counseling and Clinical Psychology, 62,* 982–988.

Jennings, N., & Wartella, E. (2004). Technology and the family. In A. L. Vangelisti (ed.), *Handbook of family communication* (pp. 593–608). Mahwah, NJ: Lawrence Erlbaum.

John, O. P., & Srivastava, S. (1999). The Big Five trait taxonomy: History, measurement, and theoretical perspective. In L. Pervin & O. John (eds), *Handbook of personality: Theory and research* (2nd edn, pp. 102–138). New York: Guilford Press.

Johnson, J., Cohen, P., Smailes, E., Kasen, S., & Brook, J. (2002). Television viewing and aggressive behavior during adolescence and adulthood. *Science, 295,* 2468–2471.

Johnson, M. P. (1995). Patriarchal terrorism and common couple violence: Two forms of violence against women. *Journal of Marriage and the Family, 57,* 283–294.

Johnson, M. P. (2008). *A typology of domestic violence: Intimate terrorism, violent resistance, and situational couple violence.* Lebanon, NH: Northeastern University Press.

Jorgenson, J. (1989). Where is the "family" in family communication? Exploring families' self-definitions. *Journal of Applied Communication Research, 17,* 27–41.

Joseph, A., & Afifi, T. (November, 2009). Military wives' stressful disclosures to their deployed husbands: The role of protective buffering. Unpublished paper presented at the National Communication Association annual meeting, Chicago, IL.

Kail, R. V., & Cavanaugh, J. C. (2007). *Human development: A life-span view* (4th edn). Belmont, CA: Thomson Higher Learning.

Karpel, M. (1980). Family secrets. *Family Processes, 19,* 295–306.

Kashy, D., Donnellan, M., Burt, A., & McGue, M. (2008). Modeling and structural equation modeling: The case of adolescent twins' conflict with their mothers. *Developmental Psychology, 44,* 316–329.

Kazdin, A. E., & Benjet, C. (2003). Spanking children: Evidence and issues. *Current Directions in Psychological Science, 12,* 99–103.

References

Kelley, D. (1999). Relational expectancy fulfillment as an explanatory variable for distinguishing couple types. *Human Communication Research, 25,* 420–442.

Kettrey, H. H., & Emery, B. C. (2006). The discourse of sibling violence. *Journal of Family Violence, 21,* 407–416.

Kirkpatrick, L. A., & Davis, K. E. (1994). Attachment style, gender, and relationship stability: A longitudinal analysis. *Journal of Personality and Social Psychology, 66,* 502–512.

Kirkpatrick, L. A., & Hazan, C. (1994). Attachment styles and close relationships: A four-year prospective study. *Personal Relationships, 1,* 123–142.

Kleban, M. H., Brody, E. M., Schoonover, C. B., & Hoffman, C. (1989). Family help to the elderly: Perceptions of sons-in-law regarding parent care. *Journal of Marriage and the Family, 51,* 303–312.

Klein, R. C. A., & Johnson, M. P. (1997). Strategies of couple conflict. In S. Duck (ed.), *Handbook of personal relationships: Theory, research, and interventions* (2nd edn, pp. 267–486). New York: Wiley.

Klonsky, E. D. (2009). The functions of self-injury in young adults who cut themselves: Clarifying the evidence for affect-regulation. *Psychiatry Research, 166,* 260–268.

Knafl, K. A. & Gilliss, C. L. (2002). Families and chronic illness: A synthesis of current research. *Journal of Family Nursing, 8,* 178–199.

Kobak, R. R., & Sceery, A. (1988). Attachment in late adolescence: Working models, affect regulation, and representations of self and others. *Child Development, 59,* 135–146.

Koerner, A. F. & Fitzpatrick, M. A. (1997). Family type and conflict: The impact of conversation orientation on conflict in the family. *Communication Studies, 48,* 59–75.

Koerner, A. F., & Fitzpatrick, M. A. (2002). Toward a theory of family communication. *Communication Theory, 12,* 70–91.

Koerner, A., & Fitzpatrick, M. (2004). Communication in intact families. In A. Vangelisti (ed.), *Handbook of family communication* (pp. 177–195). Mahwah, NJ: Lawrence Erlbaum.

Koerner, A. F., & Fitzpatrick, M. A. (2006). Family communication patterns theory: A social cognitive approach. In D. Braithwaite & L. Baxter (eds), *Engaging theories in family communication: Multiple perspectives* (pp. 50–65). Thousand Oaks, CA: Sage.

Koesten, J. (2004). Family communication patterns, sex of subject, and communication competence. *Communication Monographs, 71,* 226–244.

Koesten, J., Schrodt, P., & Ford, D. (2009). Cognitive flexibility as a mediator of family communication environments and young adults' well-being. *Health Communication, 24,* 82–94.

Kohler, J. K., Grotevant, H. D., & McRoy, R. G. (2002). Adopted adolescents' preoccupation with adoption: The impact on adoptive family relationships. *Journal of Marriage and Family, 64,* 93–104.

Konrath, S., Bushman, B., & Grove, T. (2009). Seeing my world in a million little pieces: Narcissism, self-construal, and cognitive-perceptual style. *Journal of Personality, 77*, 1197–1228.

Kowalski, R. L. (2007). Teasing and bullying. In B. Spitzberg & W. Cupach (eds), *The dark side of interpersonal communication* (2nd edn, pp. 169–197). Mahwah, NJ: Lawrence Erlbaum.

Kraut, R., Mukophadyay, T., Szczypula, J., Kiesler, S., & Scherlis, B. (2000). Information and communication: Alternative uses of the Internet in households. *Information Systems Research, 10*, 287–303.

Kraut, R. E., & Price, J. D. (1976). Machiavellianism in parents and their children. *Journal of Personality and Social Pyschology, 33*, 782–786.

Krcmar, M., & Vieira, E. T., Jr. (2005). Imitating life, imitating television: The effects of family and television models on children's moral reasoning. *Communication Research, 32*, 267–294. doi: 10.1177/0093650205275381

Kunkel, A., Hummert, M. L., & Dennis, M. R. (2006). Social learning theory: Modeling and communication in the family context. In D. Braithwaite & L. Baxter (eds), *Engaging theories in family communication: Multiple perspectives* (pp. 260–275). Thousand Oaks, CA: Sage.

La France, B. H., Heisel, A. D., & Beatty, M. J. (2004). Is there empirical evidence for a nonverbal profile of extraversion? A meta-analysis and critique of the literature. *Communication Monographs, 71*, 28–48.

Larsen, R. J., & Ketelaar, T. (1991). Personality and susceptibility to positive and negative emotional states. *Journal of Personality and Social Psychology, 61*, 132–140.

Lease, S. H. (2002). A model of depression in adult children of alcoholics and nonalcoholics. *Journal of Counseling & Development, 80*, 441–451.

Lee-Baggley, D., Preece, M., & DeLongis, A. (2005). Coping with interpersonal stress: Role of Big Five traits. *Journal of Personality, 73*, 1141–1180. doi: 10.1111/j.1467–6494.2005.00345.x.

Leonard, K. E., & Senchak, M. (1996). Prospective prediction of husband marital aggression within newlywed couples. *Journal of Abnormal Psychology, 105*, 369–380.

Le Poire, B. A. (1992). Does the codependent encourage substance dependent behavior? Paradoxical injunctions in the codependent relationship. *The International Journal of the Addictions, 27*, 1465–1474.

Le Poire, B. A. (1994). Inconsistent nurturing as control theory: Implications for communication-based research and treatment programs. *Journal of Applied Communication Research, 23*, 1–15.

Le Poire, B. A. (2004). The influence of drugs and alcohol on family communication: The effects that substance abuse has on family members and the effects that family members have on substance abuse. In A. L. Vangelisti (ed.), *Handbook of family communication* (pp. 609–628). Mahwah, NJ: Lawrence Erlbaum.

References

Le Poire, B. A. (2006). *Family communication: Nurturing and control in a changing world.* Thousand Oaks, CA: Sage.

Le Poire, B., Hallett, J., & Erlandson, K. (2000). An initial test of inconsistent nurturing as control theory: How partners of drug abusers assist their partners' sobriety. *Human Communication Research, 26*, 432–457.

Leslie, L. A., & Southward, A. L. (2009). Thirty years of feminist family therapy: Moving into the mainstream. In S. A. Lloyd, A. L. Few, & K. R. Allen (eds), *The handbook of feminist family studies* (pp. 328–339). Thousand Oaks, CA: Sage.

Levesque, C., Lafontaine, M., Bureau, J., Cloutier, P., & Dandurand, C. (2010). The influence of romantic attachment and intimate partner violence on nonsuicidal self-injury in young adults. *Journal of Youth and Adolescence, 39*, 474–483.

Levitan, S., Lloyd, C. (producers), & Winer, J. (director) (2009). *Modern family* [Television series]. USA: 20th Century Fox Television.

Levy, M. B., & Davis, K. E. (1988). Lovestyles and attachment styles compared: Their relations to each other and to various relationship characteristics. *Journal of Social and Personal Relationships, 5*, 439–471.

Littlejohn, S. W. (1999). *Theories of human communication* (6th ed.). Belmont, CA: Wadsworth.

Lloyd, S., Allen, K., & Few, A. (eds) (2009). *Handbook of feminist family studies.* Los Angeles, CA: Sage.

Lloyd, S. A., & Emery, B. (1999). *The dark side of courtship: Physical and sexual aggression.* Thousand Oaks, CA: Sage.

Loseke, D. R. (2005). Through a sociological lens: The complexities of family violence. In D. R. Loseke, R. J. Gelles, & M. M. Cavanaugh (eds), *Current controversies on family violence* (2nd edn, pp. 35–47). Thousand Oaks, CA: Sage.

Lucas, R., & Baird, B. (2004). Extraversion and emotional reactivity. *Journal of Personality and Social Psychology, 86*, 473–485.

McCabe, S. B., & Gotlib, I. H. (1993). Interactions of couples with and without a depressed spouse: Self-report and observations of problem-solving situations. *Journal of Social and Personal Relationships, 10*, 589–599.

McCarthy, B., Hagan, J., & Martin, M. J. (2002). In and out of harm's way: Violent victimization and the social capital of fictive street families. *Criminology, 40*, 831–866.

McCrae, R., & Costa, P. (1999). A five-factor theory of personality. In L. Pervin & O. John (eds), *Handbook of personality: Theory and research* (2nd edn, pp. 139–153). New York: Guilford Press.

McCubbin, M. A., & McCubbin, H. I. (1993). Families coping with illness: The resiliency model of family stress, adjustment, and ethnicity. *Family Relations, 37*, 247–254.

McDevitt, M., & Chaffee, S. (2002). From top-down to trickle-up influence: Revisiting assumptions about the family in political socialization. *Political Communication, 19*, 281–301.

References

McDevitt, M., & Ostrowski, A. (2009). The adolescent unbound: Unintentional influence of curricula on ideological conflict seeking. *Political Communication, 26*, 11–29.

McHoskey, J. W. (1999). Machiavellianism, intrinsic versus extrinsic goals, and social interest: Determination theory analysis. *Motivation and Emotion, 23*, 267–283.

Mackey, W. (1988). Patterns of adult-child associations in 18 cultures: An index of the "nuclear family." *Journal of Comparative Family Studies, 19*, 69–84.

McLeod, J. M., & Chaffee, S. H. (1972). The construction of social reality. In J. Tedeschi (ed.), *The social influence processes* (pp. 50–59). Chicago, IL: Aldine-Atherton.

Malamuth, N. M., & Check, J. V. P. (1981). The effects of mass media exposure on acceptance of violence against women: A field experiment. *Journal of Research in Personality, 15*, 436–446.

Malamuth, N. M., & Check, J. V. P. (1985). The effects of aggressive pornography on beliefs in rape myths: Individual differences. *Journal of Research in Personality, 19*, 299–320.

Marcia, J. E. (1980). Identity in adolescence. In J. Adelson (ed.), *Handbook of adolescent psychology* (pp. 159–187). New York: Wiley.

Martin, J. N., & Nakayama, T. K. (2010). *Intercultural communication in context* (5th edn). New York: McGraw-Hill.

Medved, C., Brogan, S., McClanahan, A., & Morris, J. (2006). Family and work socializing communication: Messages, gender, and ideological implications. *Journal of Family Communication, 6*, 161–180.

Medved, C., & Graham, E. (2006). Communicating contradictions: (Re) Producing dialectical tensions through work, family, and balance socialization messages. In L. Turner & R. West (eds), *The family communication sourcebook* (pp. 353–372). Thousand Oaks, CA: Sage.

Meisenbach, R., Remke, R., Buzzanell, P., & Liu, M. (2008). "They allowed": Pentadic mapping of women's maternity leave discourse as organizational rhetoric. *Communication Monographs, 75*, 1–24.

Mercer, J. (2006). *Understanding attachment: Parenting, child care, and emotional development.* Westport, CT: Praeger.

Messman, S. J., & Canary, D. J. (1998). Patterns of conflict in personal relationships. In W. R. Cupach & B. H. Spitzberg (eds), *The dark side of close relationships* (pp. 121–152). Mahwah, NJ: Lawrence Erlbaum.

Mikulincer, M., Florian, V., & Tolmacz, R. (1990). Attachment styles and fear of personal death: A case study of affect regulation. *Journal of Personality and Social Psychology, 58*, 273–280.

Mikulincer, M., & Orbach, I. (1995). Attachment styles and repressive defensiveness: The accessibility and architecture of affective memories. *Journal of Personality and Social Psychology, 68*, 917–925.

Millar, F. E., & Rogers, L. E. (1976). A relational approach to interpersonal

References

communication. In G. R. Miller (ed.), *Explorations in interpersonal communication* (pp. 87–103). Beverly Hills, CA: Sage.

Millar, F. E., Rogers, L. E., & Bavelas, J. B. (1984). Identifying patterns of verbal conflict in interpersonal dynamics. *Western Journal of Communication, 48,* 231–246.

Miller, I. W., McDermut, W., Gordon, K. C., Keitner, G. I., Ryan, C. E., & Norman, W. (2000). Personality and family functioning in depressed patients. *Journal of Abnormal Psychology, 109,* 539–545.

Miller, J. D., Campbell, W. K., Young, D. L., Lakey, C. E., Reidy, D.E., Zeichner, A., & Goodie, A. S. (2009). Examining the relations among narcissism, impulsivity, and self-defeating behaviors. *Journal of Personality, 77,* 761–794.

Miller, K. (2005). *Communication theories: Perspectives, processes, and contexts* (2nd edn). Boston, MA: McGraw-Hill.

Miller, M. & Day, L. E. (2002). Family communication, maternal and paternal expectations, and college students' suicidality. *Journal of Family Communication, 2,* 167–184.

Minuchin, S. (1984). *Family kaleidoscope.* Cambridge, MA: Harvard University Press.

Morgan, W., & Wilson, S. R. (2007). Explaining child abuse as a lack of safe ground. In W. R. Cupach & B. H. Spitzberg (eds), *The dark side of interpersonal communication* (2nd edn, pp. 327–362). Hillsdale, NJ: Lawrence Erlbaum.

Morrison, M., & Krugman, D. (2001). A look at mass and computer mediated technologies: Understanding the roles of television and computers in the home. *Journal of Broadcasting and Electronic Media, 45,* 135–161.

Murdock, P. M. (1949). *Social structure.* New York: Free Press.

Murray, J. P. (2008). Media violence: The effects are both real and strong. *American Behavioral Scientist, 51,* 1212–1230.

Myers, S. A., & Bryant, L. H. (2008). The use of behavioral indicators of sibling commitment among emerging adults. *Journal of Family Communication, 8,* 101–125.

Nakao, K., Takaishi, J., Tatsuta, K., Katayam, H., Iwase, M., Yorifuji, K., & Takeda, M. (2000). The influence of family environment on personality traits. *Psychiatry and Clinic Neurosciences, 52,* 91–95.

National Family Caregivers Association (2010, September 15). About NFCA. Retrieved from http://www.thefamilycaregiver.org/about_nfca/

National Institute of Mental Health (2007). *Eating Disorders* (NIH Publication No. 07–4901).

Nilsen, K. (2010). Invisible sister: Silence in love and loss. Presented at Western States Communication Association Annual Convention, Anchorage, AK.

Nock, M. K. (2010). Self-injury. *Annual Review of Clinical Psychology, 6,* 339–363.

Nock, M. K., & Prinstein, M. J. (2004). A functional approach to the assessment of self-mutilative behavior. *Journal of Consulting Clinical Psychology, 72,* 885–890.

Nolen-Hoeksema, S. (1987). Sex differences in unipolar depression: Evidence and theory. *Psychological Bulletin, 101,* 259–282.

Noller, P., & Feeney, J. A. (2004). Studying family communication: Multiple methods and multiple sources. In A. Vangelisti (ed.), *Handbook of family communication* (pp. 31–50). Mahwah, NJ: Lawrence Erlbaum.

Noller, P., & Fitzpatrick, M. A. (1992). *Communication in family relationships.* New York: Allyn and Bacon.

Olson, D. H. (2000). Circumplex model of marital and family systems. *Journal of Family Therapy, 22,* 144–167.

Olson, D. H., & DeFrain, J. (1997). *Marriage and the family: Diversity and strengths* (2nd edition). Mountain View, CA: Mayfield.

Olson, L. N. (2002a). Exploring "common couple violence" in heterosexual romantic relationships. *Western Journal of Communication, 66,* 104–128.

Olson, L. N. (2004). Relational control-motivated aggression: A theoretically based typology of intimate violence. *Journal of Family Communication, 4,* 209–233.

Olson, L. N. (2008). Relational control-motivated aggression: A theoretical framework for identifying various types of violent couples. In D. D. Cahn (ed.), *Family violence: Communication processes* (pp. 27–47). Albany, NY: SUNY Press.

Olson, L. N. (2009). Deviance and human relationships. In H. T. Reis & S. Sprecher (eds), *Encyclopedia of Human Relationships.* Thousand Oaks, CA: Sage.

Olson, L. N., & Golish, T. D. (2002). Topics of conflict and patterns of aggression in romantic relationships. *Southern Communication Journal, 67,* 180–200.

Olson, L. N., & Lloyd, S. A. (2005). "It depends on what you mean by starting": An exploration of how women define initiation of aggression and their motives for behaving aggressively. *Sex Roles, 53,* 603–617.

Ozer, D. J., & Benet-Martinez, V. (2006). Personality and the prediction of consequential outcomes. *Annual Review of Psychology, 57,* 401–421.

Palazzolo, K. E., Roberto, A. J., & Babin, E. A. (2010). The relationship between parents' verbal aggression and young adult children's intimate partner violence victimization and perpetration. *Health Communication, 25,* 357–364.

Paolucci, E. O., & Violato, C. (2004). A meta-analysis of the published research on the affective, cognitive, and behavioral effects of corporal punishment. *Journal of Psychology, 138,* 197–221.

Pardini, D. A., Lochman, J. E., & Powell, N. (2007). The development of callous-unemotional traits and antisocial behavior in children: Are there shared and/or unique predictors? *Journal of Clinical Child and Adolescent Psychology, 36,* 319–333.

References

Payne, M. J., & Sabourin, T. C. (1990). Argumentative skill deficiency and its relationship to quality of marriage. *Communication Research Reports, 7,* 121–124.

Pearce, L., & Thornton, A. (2007). Religious identity and family ideologies in the transition to adulthood. *Journal of Marriage and Family Therapy, 69,* 1227–1243.

Pelaez, M., Field, T., Pickens, J. N., & Hart, S. (2008). Disengaged and authoritarian parenting behavior of depressed mothers with their toddlers. *Infant Behavior & Development, 31,* 145–148.

Perry-Jenkins, M., Pierce, C., & Goldberg, A. (2004). Discourses on diapers and dirty laundry: Family communication about child care and housework. In A. Vangelisti (ed.), *Handbook of family communication* (pp. 541–561). Mahwah, NJ: Lawrence Erlbaum.

Peters, S. (1996). *The ascent of the superman.* New Haven, CT: Yale University Press.

Petronio, S. (2002). *Boundaries of privacy: Dialectics of disclosures.* Albany, NY: SUNY Press.

Petronio, S., & Durham, W. T. (2008). Communication privacy management theory: Significance for interpersonal communication. In L. A. Baxter & D. O. Braithwaite (eds), *Engaging theories in interpersonal communication: Multiple perspectives* (pp. 309–322). Thousand Oaks, CA: Sage.

Pew Internet & American Life Project (2008, July 27). Networked families. Retrieved from http://www.pewinternet.org/Reports/2008/Networked-Families.aspx?r=1

Philipsen, G. (2002). Cultural communication. In W. B. Gudykunst & B. Mody (eds), *Handbook of international and intercultural communication* (2nd edn, pp. 51–68). Thousand Oaks, CA: Sage.

Plomin, R., & Caspi, A. (1999). Behavioral genetics and personality. In L. Pervin & O. John (eds), *Handbook of personality psychology* (2nd edn, pp. 251–276). New York: Guilford Press.

Popenoe, D. (1993). American family decline, 1960–1990: A review and appraisal. *Journal of Marriage and Family, 55,* 527–555.

Postigo, J. M. L., & Honrubia, R. L. (2010). The co-residence of elderly people with their children and grandchildren. *Educational Gerontology, 36,* 330–349.

Potter, W. J. (2005). *Media literacy* (3rd edn). Thousand Oaks, CA: Sage.

Poulos, C. N. (2009). *Accident ethnography: An inquiry into family secrecy.* Walnut Creek, CA: Left Coast Press.

Prescott, M. E., & Le Poire, B. A. (2002). Eating disorders and mother-daughter communication: A test of inconsistent nurturing as control theory. *Journal of Family Communication, 2,* 59–78.

Prinzie, P., Stams, G. J. J. M., Dekovic, M., Reijntjes, A. H. A., & Belsky, J. (2009). The relations between parents' Big Five personality factors and parenting: A meta-analytic review. *Journal of Personality and Social Psychology, 97,* 351–362. doi: 10.1037/a0015823

Quote DB (2010, September 1). [Database of quotes]. Retrieved from http://www.quotedb.com/quotes/2355

RAINN (2010). *Who are the victims?* Retrieved from http://www.rainn.org/get-information/statistics/sexual-assault-victims.

Rancer, A. S., & Avtgis, T. A. (2006). *Argumentative and aggressive communication: Theory, research, and application.* Thousand Oaks, CA: Sage.

Rangarajan, S., & Kelly, L. (2006). Family communication patterns, family environment, and the impact of parental alcoholism on offspring self-esteem. *Journal of Social and Personal Relationships, 23,* 655–671.

Rhodewalt, F., Madrian, J. C., & Cheney, S. (1998). Narcissism, self-knowledge organization, and emotional reactivity: The effect of daily experiences on self-esteem and affect. *Personality and Social Psychology Bulletin, 24,* 75–87.

Rhodewalt, F., & Morf, C. C. (1998). On self-aggrandizement and anger: A temporal analysis of narcissism and affective reactions to success and failure. *Journal of Personality and Social Psychology, 74,* 672–685.

Riggio, H., & Riggio, R. (2002). Emotional expressiveness, extraversion, and neuroticism: A meta-analysis. *Journal of Nonverbal Behavior, 26,* 195–218.

Rill, L., Baiocchi, E., Hopper, M., Denker, K., & Olson, L. N. (2009). Exploration of the relationship between self-esteem, commitment, and verbal aggressiveness in romantic dating relationships. *Communication Reports, 22,* 102–113.

Ritchie, L. D., & Fitzpatrick, M. A. (1990). Family communication patterns: Measuring intrapersonal perceptions of interpersonal relationships. *Communication Research, 17,* 523–544.

Robb, J. (2008). Denver to host sodomy conference. *The Torch, 194,* 14.

Rogers, L. E. (2001). Relational communication in the context of family. *Journal of Family Communication, 1,* 25–34.

Rogers, L. E. (2004). The development of relational communication: A personal narrative. *Journal of Family Communicaiton, 4,* 157–165.

Rogers, L. E., & Millar, F. E. (1988). Relational communication. In S. Duck (ed.), *Handbook of personal relationships* (pp. 289–305). New York: Wiley.

Rogers-Millar, L. E., & Millar, F. E., III (1979). Domineeringness and dominance: A transactional view. *Human Communication, 5,* 238–246.

Rogge, R. D., Bradbury, T. N., Hahlweg, K., Engle, J., & Thurmaier, F. (2006). Predicting marital distress and dissolution: Refining the two-factor hypothesis. *Journal of Family Psychology, 20,* 156–159.

Roloff, M. E., & Cloven, D. H. (1990). The chilling effect in interpersonal relationships: The reluctance to speak one's mind. In D. D. Cahn (ed.), *Intimates in conflict: A communication perspective* (pp. 49–76). Hillsdale, NJ: Erlbaum.

Roloff, M., & Miller, C. W. (2006). Mulling about family conflict and communication: What we know and what we need to know. In L. Turner & R. West

References

(eds), *The family communication sourcebook* (pp. 143–164). Thousand Oaks, CA: Sage.

Roloff, M. E., & Soule, K. P. (2002). Interpersonal conflict: A review. In M. L. Knapp and J. A. Daly (eds), *Handbook of interpersonal communication* (pp. 475–528). Thousand Oaks, CA: Sage.

Rosemond, J. (2005). Proper socialization requires powerful love and equally powerful discipline. In D. R. Loseke, R. J. Gelles, M. M. Cavanaugh (eds), *Current controversies on family violence* (pp. 131–136). Thousand Oaks, CA: Sage.

Ross, J. M., & Babcock, J. C. (2009). Gender differences in partner violence in context: Deconstructing Johnson's (2001) control-based typology of violent couples. *Journal of Aggression, Maltreatment, & Trauma*, 604–622. doi: 10.1080/10926770903103180.

Rudman, L., & Glick, P. (2008). *The social psychology of gender: How power and intimacy shape gender relations*. New York: Guilford.

Sabourin, T. C. (2003). *The contemporary American family: A dialectical perspective on communication and relationships*. Thousand Oaks, CA: Sage.

Sahlstein, E., Maguire, K. C., & Timmerman, L. (2009). Contradictions and praxis contextualized by wartime deployment: Wives' perspectives revealed through relational dialectics. *Communication Monographs, 76*, 421–442.

Schrodt, P. (2009). Family strength and satisfaction as functions of family communication environments. *Communication Quarterly, 57*, 171–186.

Schrodt, P., Witt, P. L., & Messersmith, A. S. (2008). A meta-analytical review of family communication patterns and their associations with information processing, behavioral, and psychosocial outcomes. *Communication Monographs, 75*, 248–269.

Schwartz, S. (producer), & Rudolph, O. (director) (1969). *The Brady Bunch* [television series]. USA: Paramount Pictures Corporation.

Segrin, C. (2001). *Interpersonal processes in psychological problems*. New York: Guilford Press.

Segrin, C., Badger, T. A., Meek, P., Lopez, A. M., Bonham, E., & Sieger, A. (2005). Dyadic interdependence on affect and quality-of-life trajectories among women with breast cancer and their partners. *Journal of Social and Personal Relationships, 22*, 673–689.

Serewicz, M. C. M. (2006). Getting along with the in-laws: Relationships with parents-in-law. In K. Floyd & M. Morman (eds), *Widening the family circle: New research on family communication* (pp. 101–116). Thousand Oaks, CA: Sage.

Shearman, S., & Dumlao, R. (2008). A cross-cultural comparison of family communication patterns and conflict between young adults and parents. *Journal of Family Communication, 8*, 186–211.

Sillars, A., Canary, D. L., & Tafoya, M. (2004). Communication, conflict, and the quality of family relationships. In A. L. Vangelisti (ed.), *Handbook of family communication* (pp. 413–446). Mahwah, NJ: Lawrence Erlbaum.

Silverstein, M., & Marenco, A. (2001). How Americans enact the grandparent role across the family life course. *Journal of Family Issues, 22*, 493–522.

Singh, R. (2009). Constructing "the family" across culture. *Journal of Family Therapy, 31*, 359–383.

Smith, H. (2008). Searching for kinship: The creation of street families among homeless youth. *American Behavioral Scientist, 51*, 756–771.

Soliz, J., Thurson, A., & Rittenour, C. (2009). Communicative correlates of satisfaction, family identity, and group salience in multiracial/ethnic families. *Journal of Marriage and Family, 71*, 819–832.

Solomon, D., Knobloch, L., & Fitzpatrick, M. (2004). Relational power, marital schema, and decisions to withhold complaints: An investigation of the chilling effect on confrontation in marriage. *Communication Studies, 45*, 146–167.

Solomon, P. L., Cavanaugh, M. M., & Gelles, R. J. (2005). Violence among adults with severe mental illness: A neglected area of research. *Trauma, Violence, & Abuse, 6*, 40–54.

Spitzberg, B. H. (2000). What is good communication? *Journal of the Association for Communication Administration, 29*, 103–119.

Spitzberg, B. H., & Cupach, W. R. (1989). *The handbook of interpersonal communication competence*. New York: Springer-Verlag.

Spitzberg, B. H., & Cupach, W. R. (1994). Dark side denouement. In W. R. Cupach & B. H. Spitzberg (eds), *The dark side of interpersonal communication* (pp. 315–320). Hillsdale, NJ: Lawrence Erlbaum.

Spitzberg, B. H., & Cupach, W. R. (1998). Introduction: Dusk, detritus, and delusion: A prolegomenon to the dark side of close relationships. In W. R. Cupach & B. H. Spitzberg (eds), *The dark side of close relationships* (pp. xi–xxii). Mahwah, NJ: Lawrence Erlbaum.

Spitzberg, B. H., & Cupach, W. R. (2002). Interpersonal skills. In M. L. Knapp & J. A. Daly (eds), *The handbook of interpersonal communication* (3rd edn, pp. 564–611). Thousand Oaks, CA: Sage.

Spitzberg, B. H., & Cupach, W. R. (2007). Disentangling the dark side of interpersonal communication. In B. H. Spitzberg & W. R. Cupach (eds), *The dark side of interpersonal communication* (pp. 3–28). Mahwah, NJ: Lawrence Erlbaum.

Stacey, J. (1990). *Brave new families*. New York: Basic Books.

Stafford, L., & Dainton, M. (1994). The dark side of "normal" family interaction. In W. R. Cupach & B. H. Spitzberg (eds), *The dark side of interpersonal communication* (pp. 259–280). Hillsdale, NJ: Lawrence Erlbaum.

Stamp, G. H. (2004). Theories of family relationships and a family relationships theoretical model. In A. L. Vangelisti (ed.), *Handbook of family communication* (pp. 1–30). Mahwah, NJ: Lawrence Erlbaum.

Stamp, G., & Sabourin, T. (1995). Accounting for violence: An analysis of male spousal abuse narratives. *Journal of Applied Communication Research, 23,* 284–308.

Steil, J. M. (2000). Contemporary marriage: Still an unequal partnership. In C. Hendrick & S. S. Hendrick (eds), *Close relationships: A sourcebook* (pp. 125–136). Thousand Oaks, CA: Sage.

Stewart, A. E., & Stewart, E. A. (2006). The preference to excel and its relationship to selected personality variables. *Journal of Individual Psychology, 62,* 270–284.

Stith, S. M., Amanor-Boadu, Y., Miller, M. S., Menhusen, E., Morgan, C., & Few-Demo, A. (2011). Vulnerabilities, stressors, and adaptations in situationally violent relationships. *Family Relations, 60,* 73–89. doi: 10.1111/j.1741–3729.2010.00634.x.

Straus, M. A. (1996). Corporal punishment in America and its effect on children. *Journal of Child Centered Practice, 3,* 57–77.

Straus, M. A. (2005). Children should never, ever be spanked no matter what the circumstances. In D. R. Loseke, R. J. Gelles, M. M. Cavanaugh (eds), *Current controversies on family violence* (pp. 137–157). Thousand Oaks, CA: Sage.

Sturge-Apple, M. L., Davies, P. T., & Cummings, E. M. (2010). Typologies of family functioning and children's adjustment during the early school years. *Child Development, 81,* 1320–1335.

Taraban, C. B., Hendrick, S. S., & Hendrick, C. (1998). Loving and liking. In P. A. Andersen & L. K. Guerrero (eds), *Handbook of communication and emotion* (pp. 331–351). San Diego, CA: Academic Press.

Tevan, J. J., Martin, M. W., & Neupauer, N. C. (1998). Sibling relationships: Verbally aggressive messages and their effect on relational satisfaction. *Communication Reports, 11,* 179–186.

Thompson, L., Snyder, C. R., Hoffman, L., Michael, S. T., Rasmussen, H. N., et al. (2005). Dispositional forgiveness of self, others, and situations. *Journal of Personality, 73,* 313–359.

Thrash, T. M., & Elliot, A. J. (2004). Inspiration: Core characteristics, component processes, antecedents, and function? *Journal of Personality and Social Psychology, 87,* 957–973.

Toller, P. W. (2007). Negotiation of dialectical contradictions by parents who have experienced the death of a child. *Journal of Applied Communication Research, 33,* 46–66.

Toller, P. W. (2008). Bereaved parents' negotiation of identity following the death of a child. *Communication Studies, 59,* 306–321.

Tolstoy, L. (1873/2004). *Anna Karenina.* New York: Dover Publications.

Trull, T. J., & Sher, K. J. (1994). Relationship between the five factor model of personality and Axis I disorders in a nonclinical sample. *Journal of Abnormal Psychology, 103,* 350–360.

Tuft, C., & Holleman, J. (2000, March). *Inside the Christian Identity movement.*

Retrieved April 22, 2010 from http://www.rickross.com/reference/christian_identity/christianidentity7.html

Turner, L. H. & West, R. (1998). *Perspective on family communication*. Mountain View, CA: Mayfield.

Turner, L. H. & West, R. (2006/2002). *Perpectives on family communication* (3rd edn). New York: McGraw-Hill.

US Department of Health and Human Services (2008). *Understanding drug abuse and addition* [brochure].

Vangelisti, A. L. (1994). Family secrets: Forms, functions and correlates. *Journal of Social and Personal Relationships*, 11, 113–135.

Vangelisti, A. L. (2002). Interpersonal processes in romantic relationships. In M. L. Knapp & J. A. Daly (eds), *Handbook of interpersonal communication* (pp. 643–679). Thousand Oaks, CA: Sage.

Vangelisti, A. L. (2004). Preface. *Handbook of family communication* (pp. ix–xii). Mahwah, NJ: Lawrence Erlbaum.

Vangelisti, A. L. & Caughlin, J. P. (1997). Revealing family secrets: The influence of topic, function, and relationships. *Journal of Social and Personal Relationships*, 14, 679–705.

Vangelisti, A. L., Knapp, M. L., & Daly, J. A. (1990). Conversational narcissism. *Communication Monographs*, 57, 251–274.

Vangelisti, A. L., Maguire, K., Alexander, L., & Clark, G. (2007). Hurtful family environments: Links with individual, relationship, and perceptual variables. *Communication Monographs*, 74, 357–385.

Vangelisti, A. L., & Sprague, R. J. (1998). Guilt and hurt: Similarities, distinctions, and conversational strategies. In P. A. Andersen & L. K. Guerrero (eds), *Handbook of communication and emotion* (pp. 122–154). San Diego, CA: Academic Press.

Vermaes, I. P. R., Janssens, J. M. A. M., Mullaart, R. A., Vinck, A., & Gerris, J. R. M. (2008). Parents' personality and parenting stress in families of children with spina bifida. *Child: Care, Health and Development, 34(5)*, 665–674 doi:10.1111/j.1365–2214.2008.00868.x

Vollrath, M., Neyer, F., Ystrom, E., & Landolt, M. (2010). Dyadic personality effects on family functioning in parents of newly hospitalized children. *Personal Relationships*, 17, 27–40.

von Bertalanffy, L. (1950). An outline of general system theory. *British Journal for the Philosophy of Science, 1*, 134–165.

von Bertalanffy, L. (1968). *General systems theory*. New York: Braziller.

von Bertalanffy, L. (1972). The history and status of general systems theory. *Academy of Management Journal, 15*, 407–427.

Watzlawick, P., Bavelas, J. B., & Jackson, D. D. (1967). *Pragmatics of human communication: A study of interactional patterns, pathologies, and paradoxes*. New York: W. W. Norton.

References

Weaver, C. K., & Carter, C. (2006). Grim news. In *Critical readings: Violence and the media* (pp. 21–41). New York: Open University Press.

Weigel, D., & Ballard-Reisch, D. (2008). Relational maintenance, satisfaction, and commitment in marriages: An actor-partner analysis. *Journal of Family Communication, 8*, 212–229.

Weiner, B. (1986). *An attributional theory of motivation and emotion.* New York: Springer-Verlag.

White Pride Homeschool Resource Center (n.d.). Retrieved August 1, 2010 from http://www.whitepridehomeschool.com/

Whitty, M. T. (2007). Manipulation of self in cyberspace. In B. H. Spitzberg & W. R. Cupach (eds), *The dark side of interpersonal communication* (2nd edn, pp. 93–118). Mahwah, NJ: Lawrence Erlbaum.

Wilson, S. R., & Morgan, W. M. (2004). Persuasion and families. In A. L. Vangelisti (ed.), *Handbook of family communication* (pp. 447–472). Mahwah, NJ: Lawrence Erlbaum.

Wisdom Quotes (2010a, September 1) [family quotes]. Retrieved from http://www.wisdomquotes.com/topics/family/

Wisdom Quotes (2010b, September 1) [family quotes]. Retrieved from http://meaningfulnicesayings.com/family.php

Wood, J. (2007). *Gendered lives: Communication, gender, and culture* (7th edn). Belmont, CA: Thomson Wadsworth.

Wood, J. (2011). *Gendered lives: Communication, gender, and culture* (9th edn). Boston, MA: Wadsworth.

World Health Organization (2010, October 5). Depression [Explanation of depression]. Retrieved from http://www.who.int/mental_health/management/depression/definition/en/

Yllo, K. A. (2005). Through a feminist lens: Gender, diversity, and violence: Extending the feminist framework. In D. R. Loseke, R. J. Gelles, & M. M. Cavanaugh (eds), *Current controversies on family violence* (2nd edn, pp. 19–34). Thousand Oaks, CA: Sage.

Young, S. L., & Bippus, A. M. (2001). Does it make a difference if they hurt you in a funny way? Humorously and non-humorously phrased hurtful messages in personal relationships. *Communication Quarterly, 91*, 35–52.

Zelinski, J. M., & Larsen, R. J. (1999). Susceptibility to affect: A comparison of three different personality taxonomies. *Journal of Personality, 67*, 761–791.

Zimbardo, P. G. (1992). *Psychology and life* (13th edn). New York: HarperCollins.

Zimmerman, T. S., Haddock, S. A., Current, L., & Ziemba, S. (2003). Intimate partnership: Foundation to the successful balance of family and work. *American Journal of Family Therapy, 31*, 107–124.

Index

Index

Index

on diverse family forms, 124
on future influence of technology,
	122
gambling, 38–9
gender issues and differences
	conflict handling in committed
		couples, 58, 60, 62–3, 65
	and depression, 37–8
	female genital cutting, 102
	and religious and political beliefs,
		106
Gershoff, E. T., 71
Gilbert, N. W., 44
Golish, T. D., 58
Goodie, A. S., 36
Gottman, J. M.
	on demand/withdraw pattern, 63
	on emotional expression in families,
		70
	on family violence, 46
	on marital conflict, 58, 59–61
	research methods, 126
grandparents, 120
Greenberg, J. R., 35
Grodie, A. S., 36
Grotevant, H. D., 85
grounded theory, 127, 128
Grove, T., 34
Grych, J. H., 70
Gunter, B., 104–5

Haley, Alex, 1
Hallett, J., 39
Haritatos, J., 31–2
Harrison, J., 104–5
Hazan, C., 43, 44
health
	and agreeableness, 33
	and family well-being, 126
Heavy, C. L., 62
Herron, K., 47
Holman, T. B., 61
Holtzworth-Munroe, A., 46–7
homelessness, 124–5, 128
homosexuality and homosexual
	relationships, 60, 108
Hooven, C., 70

Hopper, M., 50
Horowitz, L. M., 44, 45
Hunter, M. A., 35
Huston, T. L., 63

Ickes, W., 31
identity
	bi-cultural, 31–2
	foreclosure identity status, 31
	identity construction and families, 1
illness, 120, 128
incest, 85
Inconsistent Nurturing as Control
	(INC) theory, 38–9
individuals
	attachment theory, 42–5
	impact on family communication,
		15–16, 24–55
	process of relating to others, 42
intentionality, 12–13
interaction structures
	dyadic, 16, 56–82
	family, 16, 82–98
	individual, 15–16, 24–55
	social, 16–17, 99–114
interdependence, 84–5
Internet
	influence on family communication,
		122–3
	predators, 120
interpersonal skills *see* communication
	patterns and styles
intraversion *see* extraversion

Jacobson, N. S., 46, 63
Japanese families, 101
jealousy, books about, viii
Jensen, V., 75
Johnson, M. P., 62, 65–6, 68
Joseph, A., 122
Journal of Marriage and Family, 123

Kail, R. V., 26
Katz, L. F., 70
Kelley, D., 65
Kelly, L., 30
Kettrey, H. H., 75

Index